"Rachel Hershenberg writes with authority and compassion as she presents the best techniques for moving toward a life we love. For years I've been writing about these principles and using them in my clinical practice, and still I learned a tremendous amount from *Activating Happiness* about the best ways to help people get unstuck. I also benefited personally from this powerful and practical book, as countless readers no doubt will, too."

—**Seth J. Gillihan, PhD**, author of *Retrain Your Brain: Cognitive Behavioral Therapy in 7 Weeks*

"In her delightfully written and easy-to-read book, *Activating Happiness*, Rachel Hershenberg, a talented psychotherapist and depression researcher, offers five basic principles for counteracting low motivation, depression, or feeling stuck. The book is rich with strategies and techniques that people will find enormously doable, helpful, and effective when they feel depressed or want to prevent a downward depressive spiral. Readers of the book will quickly appreciate Hershenberg's encouragement to engage in activities that truly matter, savor the experiences, and use them to create the life one desires to lead. By following the evidence-based yet very practical recommendations and using the structured activities offered in the book, people will find themselves living a more value-driven, meaningful, productive, and enjoyable life."

—**Nadine J. Kaslow, PhD, ABPP**, professor and vice chair in the department of psychiatry and behavioral sciences at Emory University, and past president (2014) of the American Psychological Association

"Rachel Hershenberg has decoded the latest science to uncover a secret that's easy to miss: to beat depression, it's not enough just to control negative emotions—you have to instill positive emotions as well. In *Activating Happiness*, Hershenberg walks you through several simple and doable strategies that just may be the step you've been missing in your battle with depression, low motivation, apathy, or other negative mood states. Take her advice to heart; your emotions will thank you for it."

—**David F. Tolin, PhD, ABPP**, author of *Face Your Fears* and *Doing CBT*

"In *Activating Happiness*, Rachel Hershenberg sets a new standard for self-help books. Writing in a style that is both highly informative and cleverly engaging, Hershenberg is able to demystify the behavioral, cognitive, and interpersonal processes that can 'lock' people into depressive states, and provide a step-wise guide to a way out of the darkness. This is psychoeducation at its best!"

—**Michael Thase, MD**, professor of psychiatry at Perelman School of Medicine at the University of Pennsylvania and physician at the Philadelphia Veterans Affairs Medical Center

"In *Activating Happiness*, Hershenberg provides a treasure trove of simple tips and strategies, along with examples and exercises for enhancing well-being that are based on heavily researched, cutting-edge scientific principles. The chapters are thoughtfully sequenced to teach practical skills, one step at a time, which can then be integrated together to address some of the most common issues that many of us struggle with at various points in our lives. A great resource—for both mental health providers' self-help resource libraries and for the providers themselves!"

—**Simon A. Rego, PsyD, ABPP**, chief psychologist and associate professor of clinical psychiatry and behavioral sciences at Albert Einstein College of Medicine/Montefiore Medical Center in New York, NY

Activating Happiness

A Jump-Start Guide *to* Overcoming Low Motivation, Depression, *or* Just Feeling Stuck

RACHEL HERSHENBERG, PhD

New Harbinger Publications, Inc.

Publisher's Note

This publication is designed to provide accurate and authoritative information in regard to the subject matter covered. It is sold with the understanding that the publisher is not engaged in rendering psychological, financial, legal, or other professional services. If expert assistance or counseling is needed, the services of a competent professional should be sought.

Distributed in Canada by Raincoast Books

Copyright © 2017 by Rachel Hershenberg
New Harbinger Publications, Inc.
5674 Shattuck Avenue
Oakland, CA 94609
www.newharbinger.com

Cover design by Amy Shoup

Acquired by Ryan Buresh

Edited by Jennifer Holder

FSC
www.fsc.org
MIX
Paper from
responsible sources
FSC® C011935

Library of Congress Cataloging-in-Publication Data on file

19   18   17

10   9   8   7   6   5   4   3   2   1   First Printing

This book is dedicated to the Veterans of the Be-Active and Be-Active Alumni groups. You brought these principles to life and touched my heart.

Contents

Foreword

When asked to write a foreword to this book, the question I immediately asked myself was whether the field needs still another self-help book. So many have been written over the years, covering all sorts of topics. In my opinion, it is very hard to write a good self-help book. What is needed is a topic that is relevant and important to many readers; a broad and deep knowledge of the evidence that exists in the field; good clinical sense and experience; and the unique ability to communicate to the reader. Dr. Hershenberg has all this in her book, and she has been able to translate what we know professionally about how people change and present it in a clear, compassionate, person-to-person dialogue with the reader. This unique self-help book has all these many qualities and more. It is not only good—it is very good.

Over the past fifty years, cognitive behavioral therapy (CBT) has created a major revolution in the field of psychotherapy. Different from psychodynamic therapy, which essentially was based on clinical observation and experience, CBT has its roots in both research and clinical observation. The research makes use of basic information about how we as humans think, feel, and act, and it provides evidence of how this can all be put together in successful clinical treatments. What the research has shown is that CBT works in helping individuals deal with problematic emotions, such as anxiety and depression, and improve not only their interpersonal functioning but also their views of themselves. In my own professional situation, where I have spent over fifty years teaching and supervising clinical psychologists, conducting research on psychotherapy, and practicing CBT, I feel confident that treatment works when I see it in the research literature and when I see it clinically. In essence, research and clinical observation provide converging views of how to understand the problems that we face as human beings and how they may be remedied through therapeutic intervention.

Dr. Hershenberg has taken some of the important advances in CBT and presented the reader with guidelines and tools to better identify and act on their needs; overcome procrastination and increase productivity; reduce the feelings of stress and depression; and learn to feel good. With these tools, she helps readers become their own therapists.

An important question is whether or not a self-help book can replace actual face-to-face psychotherapy. In some instances, it may. The real advantage of this book by Dr. Hershenberg is that it reads almost as if she is talking directly to the reader in a therapeutic interaction. Her knowledge of research, her clinical sensitivity, and her ability to communicate is what makes this an invaluable book. I can easily see its advantage, not only as a stand-alone approach to helping individuals with varying life problems but also as a supplement that therapists may use to enhance their clinical effectiveness.

At this point, however, we need full disclosure. Dr. Hershenberg was trained at Stony Brook University, and I was involved in her professional development. Am I biased? Absolutely! However, what I need to add is that I am also most proud to have been her teacher and clinical supervisor, and I am proud that she has written this very important self-help book.

—Marvin R. Goldfried, PhD
Distinguished Professor
Psychology Department
Stony Brook University
Stony Brook, NY 11794-2500

Introduction

On a daily basis, do you find yourself saying "I should be…"

- Getting to work earlier

- Going to the gym

- Procrastinating less

- Eating healthier

- Taking time to call my best friend

- Doing more to take care of myself

- And so on?

You want to do this activity. Maybe you want to engage in it because it is consistent with your values, it will bring you satisfaction, or you will experience peace of mind after doing it. Perhaps this activity will challenge you as a person or help you feel connected to others. Your wise self knows it's a healthy thing to do. Yet you make inconsistent efforts to do it, perhaps in bits and spurts. Consequently, your perennial to-do list hovers, waiting for resolution that never comes. Often the gap between what you say and what you do is bigger than you'd like to admit.

You may have a very difficult time following through on your goals, especially if you feel depressed. Perhaps you even gave up on making goals. You might be canceling plans, keeping to yourself, spending more time watching TV, escaping through the Internet, and procrastinating on whatever takes more effort than the bare minimum.

Without a doubt, opting out of your typical routine and only doing the bare minimum helps ease the pressure you feel in the moment. But you also start a vicious cycle: as you do less, your to-do list grows longer, stress accumulates, and more stress makes it even harder to get going again. With this tactic, you lose opportunities to experience moments that make you feel good—even for a few seconds or a few minutes. To make matters worse, you may criticize yourself for being lazy, feel confused about what is happening, or feel guilty for not caring like you used to.

You probably picked up this book because you feel too stuck, depressed, paralyzed, or busy to change your status quo. You may be frustrated because your daily choices are not serving you well. You may be struggling with low motivation or energy. This is a universal challenge that plagues so many of us: to fight the urge to say, "I'll do it later."

What to Expect in This Book

Activating Happiness can help you break the cycles of habits that keep you stuck, while addressing the fact that getting up and going again is *way* easier said than done. You will learn skills to help you function alongside—or in spite of—feelings of depression. In so doing, you can slowly bridge the gap between your current behavior and what you'd like to see yourself accomplish. The result is that you will create more moments of joy and meaning in your life.

This book will teach you ways to effectively navigate the everyday malaise that makes it tough to show up to the gym after a long day at work, turn off a favorite TV show so you go to bed at a reasonable hour, and pick up the phone to invite your friend to dinner. These methods will be useful if you feel depressed right now or if you want to prevent falling into a depressive episode in the future. Just as depressive habits can keep you feeling stuck and down, the routine wellness habits offered in this book can help prevent a sad mood or stressful day from growing bigger than it needs to be. A daily structure and a commitment to goals will keep you treating your mind and body right, and can prevent an everyday dip from triggering depressive habits that drain your mood even further.

The heart of this book is devoted to helping you spend time doing what matters to you. Over time, these nourishing moments accumulate to build the life you want to live. The principles will help you anticipate excuses and procrastination, which come all too easily when you're in a physical state like exhaustion or an emotional state like sadness or anger. The principles will help you catch that moment when you are tempted to take a step away from, rather than closer to, your goals.

As you practice making steady progress toward your goals, you will spend more time acting in alignment with what you value. In turn, these choices promote uplifting moments of contentment and joy, and help you view your life as meaningful. The principles will also teach you to strengthen relationships and stay on the path to wellness by celebrating your accomplishments with others.

Activating Happiness will help you build meaningful moments in your daily life by guiding you through five principles. These chapters are offered as a sequential path to guide you one step at a time.

Principle 1: Approach Rather Than Avoid

Identifying and showing up for what matters can help you cultivate seconds, minutes, or hours of positive emotions. It increases your sense that life has meaning and purpose. *What matters to you?*

This principle will help you identify your top values at this stage in your life, which paves the way for setting specific goals throughout the remainder of the book. Once you identify your priorities and decide to show up for them, you will learn to track the impact on your emotional experience. This tracking is valuable because activities that lead to positive emotional experiences are usually the activities that get repeated, whereas activities that lead to negative emotional experiences are the ones you will be tempted to avoid over and over again. When you learn to track how activities impact you, you can plan and strategize more wisely.

Principle 2: Self-Care Leaves More Energy to Engage in Activities You Value

When you are trying to get yourself to do something "optional"—that is, it can be postponed to another day—are you really going to do it if you're exhausted, hungover, hungry, or completely overwhelmed? When you are depressed or struggle with low motivation, excuses are wolves in sheep's clothing—enemies disguised as friends. They offer easy ways to say, "I couldn't possibly do that now."

In contrast, regular routines for basic self-care provide you with physical and emotional energy, promote your ability to think clearly, and help you choose wisely. When you want to tackle life goals that are technically optional, yet are consistent with your values, you will be more poised to follow through if you first energize your body and your mind.

This principle is devoted to building healthy habits for sleeping, exercising, eating, watching your substance intake, and relaxing. These behaviors then smooth the path to meeting other life goals. While a side benefit, I do want to point out that these habits have an inherently antidepressant effect.

Principle 3: Procrastination Is an Emotional Decision to Avoid Discomfort

The moments when you say "I'll take care of it later" are moments when you turn away from your goal, and typically happen because you're trying to avoid some type of discomfort. In the short term, these ubiquitous microprocrastinations make you feel more comfortable. Problem is, when you delay, delay, delay, then stress or guilt can pile on and, more to the point, you don't accomplish what you seek to accomplish.

It's helpful to understand those moments when you want to do something like clean the garage, then decide to do it tomorrow and instead read news headlines on your phone. The thinking that leads to this choice happens quickly, so I will help you break it down. Soon you'll be able to identify the emotions that get kicked up, drive the decision, and lead you to avoid, delay, or put off to another day. In this principle, you will gain awareness of your habitual "flee" button, practice hitting "pause," and cope more flexibly with discomfort so that you don't automatically throw your plans out the window. You'll learn ways of dealing with tough emotions that *don't* create more stress in your life and *don't* lead to behaviors that are antithetical to your goals. With practice, you will be prepared to tackle roadblocks you ran into with your self-care goals in Principle 2. You'll also learn to anticipate and cope with situations that can interfere with Principle 4.

Principle 4: When Your Schedule Is Full, You Do More

As you identify daily activities you'd like to accomplish, you will more successfully follow through if you have them planned on a calendar. A vague idea about how to spend a day is an invitation to get lost in YouTube videos and Wikipedia searches. By planning activities ahead of time and scheduling when you'll do them, you harness a core component of productivity. The less you have to do, the less you do. The busier you are, the more efficient and productive you are.

In this principle, you'll draw upon your values to brainstorm additional activities that you can schedule. Then you'll learn to plan and track your activities. And because showing up for what you planned is easier said than done, you will use skills from earlier principles, as well as some new ones, to increase the likelihood of successful follow-through.

Principle 5: Stay On Track by Sharing Momentary Victories

Throughout the book, you will accumulate moments when you do what you said you were going to do. It is crucial to pay attention to these times when you put your best interests into practice. Doing so minimizes the perceived discrepancy between your actual self and your ideal self. When you recognize that your behavior is different—in a healthy way—and you celebrate it with someone you trust and care about, you receive these added benefits:

- Being energized by the conversation itself

- Remembering the success happened because you told someone about it

- Gaining more perspective on the significance of the situation

- Feeling closer to the person you told

In this principle, you'll learn to celebrate your positive life events, no matter how big or small, with others. I'll describe what the conversation can sound like when it is optimally supportive. It's also important to anticipate *who* will be most supportive and *when* he or she might be most supportive. By considering the person and circumstance, you can ensure that you are turning to someone in a way that maximizes the experience for you and keeps you energized to continue tackling your valued life goals.

Exercises and Downloadable Forms

To help you integrate what you are learning into your daily life, I have included many guided exercises and methods that you can use to consider topics more deeply and also to monitor your experience. You can keep a journal with you as you read and do the exercises in there, whether on paper or electronically. You can also access copies to download and print out from the publisher's website by visiting http://www.newharbin ger.com/39430. See the back of this book for more details.

The Research Base

This is meant to be a user-friendly book. The principles and suggestions distill a rich line of psychological research. They are derived most heavily from general principles of behavior change and specific strategies from an effective treatment referred to as *behavioral activation*. Countless studies have accumulated to show that bringing intentionality to your actions, in an effort to show up for what matters, can enhance well-being generally and depression specifically.[1] Moreover, as Alex Korb's book *The Upward Spiral* summarizes, emerging research elucidates the neuroscience behind this treatment approach.[2] We now understand how the downward, negative spirals of sad mood and avoidance keep you stuck. Principle 3 is designed to help pull you out of this cycle. We also understand more about the upward spiral, in which one small behavior leads to a positive emotional experience, which makes it just a little easier to engage in the next upward behavior, and on and on. Principles 1, 2, 4, and 5 are designed to help you do just that.

There is strong empirical literature behind each of the principles. I sequenced the chapters to reflect the experience I gained by working with hundreds of patients struggling with depression and motivation. This work taught me that getting active is easier said than done. It makes sense on paper, but is difficult to put into practice. I draw from this understanding to teach skills in a way that will help you build success, one step at a time.

I've included personal examples in the journey because I want to communicate that fighting the urge to procrastinate is universally hard. I've just accumulated years of practice living the principles in this book, which helps me bridge my own gap between what I plan and what I do. In this way, it's a pleasure to share my quirky examples along the way to help you nourish yourself with meaningful moments in your day-to-day life.

From start to finish, this book will teach you to identify micromoments that brighten your mood, if ever so slightly. It offers ways to function alongside sadness and, in so doing, to slowly create more joy and meaning in the long run. I teach you to learn from your uplifting moments and to continue identifying and engaging in behaviors that will help you feel better and build the life you want. Activating happiness starts now.

Principle 1 Approach Rather Than Avoid

Here is an example of a classic avoidance scenario.

- It's 8 a.m. and you say, "I'll be home from work before 6 p.m. today and it'll still be light out. I'll run in the neighborhood then."

- At 5:45 p.m. when you return home, you say, "I'm too tired. I'll run tomorrow."

And this is an example of a way to approach the same scenario.

- At 8 a.m. you say, "I'll be home from work before 6 p.m. today and it'll still be light out. I'll run in the neighborhood then."

- You return home at 5:45 p.m. and say, "I'm tired. I don't want to run. I'll just change clothes and go outside. If I'm really so tired, I'll walk most of the way."

Rather than avoiding something that matters to you, like exercise, you can learn to approach it. When you identify and show up for activities that matter to you, you are approaching them. Doing so cultivates seconds, minutes, or hours of positive emotions—which increases your sense that life has meaning and purpose. Even if you're feeling depressed, this consonance between your values and your actions will bring benefits.

Your Values Bring Clarity

What do you value? Answering this question will help you weigh decisions and take action. While it's natural to think about values when you face big life decisions, like whether or not to move cities for a new job, in this book I encourage you to consider your values for mundane decisions you face every day. For example, do you participate in an improvisation class even though the idea makes you nervous? If there is a time conflict, do you agree to meet a friend for dinner or do you stick with your planned yoga class? Being clear on your values helps you make these kinds of grey-area decisions, when there is no clear right or wrong. There are three types of situations in which having clarity on values can help you.

Approach–Avoidance Conflict

In this situation, you are considering whether to approach, or avoid, an activity because there are both appealing and not-so-appealing qualities. In the case of the improvisation class, you want to show up but you're also terrified. If you value challenging yourself, learning a new skill, or increasing opportunities to socialize, then you might want to show up despite the fear.

Approach–Approach Conflict

When there are two attractive situations happening at the same time, or you can't do both for some reason, which good option do you choose? While going to dinner would be socially enjoyable, choosing the yoga class would help you sleep better that night. Looking to your values can aid the decision. If increasing intimacy in your friendships is a top value, you may choose the social option. If promoting your physical health is a top value, you might prefer to stick with the yoga class.

Avoidance–Avoidance Conflict

This situation feels like being caught between a rock and a hard place when you are trying to identify which is the least-bad option. Sticking to your values can help you prioritize which path to take. If you feel ill, but despise doctors, are you going to pick up the phone to make an appointment? On one hand, you will feel sick and the illness may become worse if untreated. On the other hand, you will need to endure the awkwardness of the visit and perhaps some tests. You value your well-being and having the energy to keep up with life, so you decide to call the doctor.

What Do You Value?

Knowing your values helps you identify when it's especially important to catch your urge to procrastinate and show up nevertheless. As you read through the values domains below, you may start to notice that some areas were values earlier in your life but are not high priority right now. Others may be areas you are about to prioritize for the first time. Focus on identifying your values for the short-term future, the next 6 to 12 months. We will focus on this period throughout the book so you can start to make headway on immediately relevant priorities.

Take note of whether your top values are exclusively self-oriented, focused on your own growth and development. Or perhaps they are exclusively other-oriented, more focused on relationships or the needs of others. Or maybe there's a combination. A focus on *self* versus *other* typically fluctuates throughout the course of life, and there is no magical balance. That said, if you find yourself leaning mostly one way or the other, you might want to check in with your intuitive self and ask: "Would prioritizing more balance be helpful on my path to improved well-being?" Perhaps you have not been prioritizing meaningful relationships or have been avoiding relationships completely. Alternatively, you could be so busy saying yes to others that your own health is being sacrificed.

Another thing to keep in mind is that values are different from goals. It might be your value to be a loving parent. A goal is how this value gets enacted, which technically you could check off on your to-do list. Goals for this value might include "Give my son more hugs" or "Take time to help my daughters with their homework." For now, focus on the values. You will turn these into specific action-based goals in Principle 4 as you fill your calendar with meaningful activities.

Identifying Values

To identify your values, consider the next 6 to 12 months. In a journal or on the downloadable form, write down your answer to each of these questions. Skip any that feel irrelevant.

- What type of romantic partner do you want to be? Are you involved in a romantic relationship? If not, do you want to be? And if yes, why are you in this relationship?

- What type of parent do you want to be?

- What type of son or daughter do you want to be?

- What type of family member do you want to be?

- What do you value in friendship?

- What do you value about your own education and training? Are there areas you'd like to learn more about or skills you'd like to develop?

- What type of boss or employee do you want to be? What values do you have about your role in the work environment? Do you value productivity, integrity, approachability, or other aspects of your job?

- What contribution would you like to make to the larger community? Do you value giving back, helping others, being politically involved, or other aspects of community participation?

- What does spirituality mean to you? What values do you have about the role of religion or spirituality in your life?

- What values do you have related to your physical health and emotional well-being?

- What does it mean to value self-care? Is this something you value? Why or why not?

The Well-Being Balance

Consider how your balance tips one way or another. Do you live consistent with your values or inconsistent with your values? Use the following scale to assess how often you act in accord with them. As you work through this book, your responses may change, so you can download a worksheet version of this activity at http:www.newharbinger.com/39430.

0% consistent   100% consistent
with values   with values

With your answer in mind, ask yourself the following questions.

- Does where you fall on the scale influence how you feel?

- Does it influence how you view yourself?

- Does it influence how connected you feel with others?

- How does it tie into your motivation for participating in this book?

- What do you imagine yourself following through on that would be part of your well-being recipe?

Your Top Values

After working through the questions, choose the top three values that you would like to focus on for the next 6 to 12 months. Make sure to jot them down in your journal or on the downloadable form. This list will help you prioritize which choices to stick to your guns about in the chapters to come. When you find yourself debating "Should I do X?" or "Should I do Y?" you can ask if either is consistent with one of your top values and use that information to weigh whether or not to gently push yourself to approach the activity you value.

Tracking Your Emotional Responses to Activities

Though it helps to intellectually know that an activity is consistent with your values, it's probably not enough motivation to change your behavior. When you also start to pay attention, in a systematic way, to how the choice to approach or avoid affects your physical or emotional state, then the decision-making process becomes a little more intuitive the next time and you can more easily understand your urges to procrastinate.

- If a valued activity led to a mixed bag of negative and positive emotional experiences (working out was miserable until you finished, but then you felt great), you'll probably have the urge to avoid it next time around. Anticipating this can help you plan it in a less stressful way (you always hate exercising in the morning, so you schedule it at night). Or you could schedule it in a way that facilitates showing up (you make a commitment to a gym buddy that you'll pick them up on the way and exercise together so it's more fun).

- If an avoidance activity wasn't so enjoyable (you flipped channels on the TV endlessly looking for something to watch instead of working out), that might help you remind yourself that collapsing on the couch isn't actually a good alternative.

- If the valued activity led to a positive emotional experience, you may be able to fight the urge to procrastinate in the future.

Here's the rub. When you're struggling with low motivation or depression—even if you enjoyed the valued activity—your default mode is to remember that it didn't go well. You'll anticipate that doing it again in the future will be full of effort, and therefore it won't feel worth doing. The thing is, when you actually *do* show up, well-chosen activities tend to feel better than expected, maybe even enjoyable, relaxing, or fun. So it's vital to capture, in the moment, how you feel so your future self can remember it more accurately. You can use these documented, in-the-moment ratings to guide your decisions in the next hour, day, week, and so on.

You can easily and effectively track your changing emotional experiences in everyday life using the graph in Figure 1. This encourages you to think about the different emotions you experience in terms of varying levels of *arousal* and *valence*.

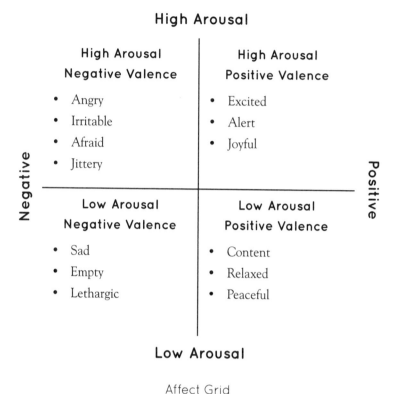

Affect Grid

Noticing High or Low Arousal

To consider your arousal level, notice how much activity is going on in your body. Is your heart pounding, are your palms sweaty, did your eyes go wide, are you alert? That's *high arousal,* which you can refer to as "H." The opposite end of the spectrum is *low arousal,* which you can refer to as "L." You may notice your heart rate is steady, you are moving or thinking more slowly, and you feel sleepy, relaxed, or sluggish.

Noticing Positive or Negative Valence

While it's important to keep in mind that no emotion is good or bad—even if it stinks to feel a certain way—it's helpful to consider the valence; that is, how positive or negative it is. The valence indicates what an emotion is communicating to you about your environment. Emotions form the basis of our survival. They communicate critical information that can get us to act quickly, build social resources and creativity, keep us out of danger's way, maintain our motivation to engage in the work we need to do to stay alive, and know when to shut down and conserve energy when the environment isn't reaping what we are sowing.

If something is *positively valenced,* or "P," it's telling you something is right and safe in your environment. You may feel emotions like excitement, joy, or relaxation. If you feel *negatively valenced,* or "N," something is telling you the situation may be dangerous or your goals are being blocked. You may feel emotions like sadness, fear, or anger.

Mapping Your Experience

With awareness of arousal and valence, you can easily do emotional check-ins by asking yourself if you are H or L—*high* or *low* arousal, and if you are P or N—*positive* or *negative* valence. These elements combine to produce four possibilities, described here as prototypical experiences.

HP: excited or alert

HN: angry, irritable, afraid, or jittery

LP: content, relaxed, or peaceful

LN: sad, empty, or lethargic

Clarifying Similar States

Two high arousal emotions or two low arousal emotions can feel similar in your body, so at first they can be confused. Are you feeling nervous or are you feeling excited? Are you feeling sad or are you feeling relaxed? Accordingly, being aware of the valence can help clarify and identify what, precisely, you are feeling.

Consider what you experience in your body when you are nervous before an annual review meeting, and what you experience when you are excited because the person you're dating sent you a text message. The physical experience might seem similar: speedy heart rate, quickened breathing, fluttery feelings. But the valence is different. You're on a threat alert with the meeting and know you're feeling nervous because you fear being negatively evaluated. In contrast, you experience the opposite with the love interest, as you are open and curious about what will happen next. You know you're feeling excited because you're thinking this person might like you back and you look forward to connecting more.

How would you code yourself right now? Throughout this book, I'll encourage you to pay attention to how your emotional experiences fluctuate throughout a day and how your behavioral choices lead to different emotional experiences. By the end of the book, you'll be a pro at identifying your current emotional state.

Acting on Your Values and Tracking the Emotional Effects

Now that you are clear on your top values, you can use them to gain a general sense of what activities you want to approach and not avoid. You also have a language for observing how your daily choices impact your emotions. With this foundation you can start to experiment in a small, but still important, way.

Is there an activity you are dreading because it feels like a lot of effort—even if it's consistent with your values and intellectually makes sense to do? What's coming up on your schedule tomorrow or later this week that you suspect you'll procrastinate doing? For this first practice, pick something pretty minor. The point is simply to begin gaining insight into these processes.

- Choose an activity to track. Maybe you'd like to make your bed before work or call your grandmother on the drive home from work.

- When the scheduled day for the activity comes around, encourage yourself to test it out. Do the activity so that you can note what happens to your emotional state. Using the H or L arousal and P or N valence ratings, code how you feel during the act. And then consider how you feel afterward.

- When it's natural to repeat the activity, try it again. The more data points you have, the more reliable your observations will be. Engage and code your emotional state.

- Rinse and repeat.

- Take note of any observations. If a behavior repeatedly leads to HP or LP states, even for a few seconds or minutes, then you may intuitively decide that it's worth the effort to plan that behavior into your days. You may also find that it starts to feel easier to resist the pull to procrastinate, since you see that the activity consistently takes you to a helpful or healthy state of mind.

This experience is the foundation for the other principles in this book. Everything that comes after this point will build on the snapshot you witnessed as you tried this process on for size. As the principles build on each other, you will be able to apply this to a full range of challenging moments that you may face on your journey to meeting your valued goals.

You are ready to progress to Principle 2. This next chapter walks you through daily habits that are universally beneficial. These habits will help give you the physical and emotional bandwidth to tackle your values-guided activities that are the heart of Principle 4. I sequenced the chapters in this way to make the journey more manageable, so that you gain practice taking care of yourself and feel just a touch calmer and healthier before engaging other goals down the road in Principle 4.

Let's turn to focusing on activities that are likely to be good for your body and mind, which are tremendous building blocks that boost your success as you pursue additional valued activities in the chapters to come.

Principle 2

Self-Care Generates More Energy to Engage in Activities You Value

Regular routines for basic self-care promote your ability to think clearly and give you the physical and emotional energy to tackle additional life goals. When you're not exhausted, hungover, hungry, or overwhelmed, you're more likely to follow through—rather than procrastinate—on an activity that could trigger a positive emotional experience. If you want a better job, you're more likely to write a cover letter when you don't have a headache from last night's outing, you're not sleep deprived, and you're not experiencing a sugar crash from candy you snacked on the hour before. With good self-care, you're more likely to write the letter, which leads to a sense of accomplishment.

In this chapter, I focus on creating healthy habits for sleep, exercise, eating, managing substances, and relaxation. Many of these beneficial behaviors are, on their own, inherently antidepressant. If you are sitting at home feeling LN or HN, a relaxation practice like diaphragmatic breathing or some physical exercise like a walk around the block might directly move you into an LP or HP emotional state.

If you have a history of depression and are using this book to stay well, I want to stress the importance of building these healthy habits because they are crucial to reducing depression relapse. When you have a bad day, a sad day, a *What is happening to my life?* kind of day, these habits provide sources of structure that keep you on a road to wellness. Continuing to adhere to your routine times for self-care helps a bump in the road remain just a bump in the road. Halting your routines is what makes you vulnerable to feeling LN or HN, which in turn makes you more vulnerable to viewing the situation as a bigger stressor than it already is. This leads to engaging in behaviors that might shoot you in the foot down the road, like getting in an argument because you're feeling irritable or avoiding things that need your attention because you're feeling too overwhelmed. In this way, a structured weekly routine is a prophylactic measure you can take to get through hard times without letting them get the best of you—and minimize the likelihood of triggering a depressive episode.

Self-Care Routines You Can Set a Clock By

We all have circadian rhythms, or clocks, which are physiological processes that correspond roughly to a 24-hour cycle. External cues in the environment signal to your body that it's time to wake up and its time to sleep throughout this 24-hour cycle. Historically, the most important environmental cue was the sun—waking with the rising sun and sleeping with the setting sun. In modern society, there are a host of other things that set, or synchronize, your circadian clock. All types of daily cues have an influence. The timing of your meals, work schedule, exercise, and TV watching can all tell your body that it's time to wake or rest.

Inconsistent cues can interfere with your circadian clock, which interferes with neurohormonal events like your daily secretion of cortisol and melatonin. These are regulating hormones, so messing with them can influence levels of energy, alertness, and appetite. When disrupted, some people bounce back right away. Others don't bounce back as easily—especially if you have a family or personal history of depression or bipolar disorder, which includes the lows of depression and the highs of mania. If you have this history, the hormonal shifts and subsequent changes in energy and appetite can put you at risk to trigger a manic or depressive episode.

You can work with your own circadian rhythm as you create new habits, since you will be most successful if you create a daily routine that is repetitive, and therefore, predictable. Synchronizing activities with your own 24-hour cycle will improve your mood and set you up to be resilient. This includes establishing routine times for sleeping and waking, eating, exercising, being active, and relaxing. Predictable self-care habits can get you on the path to having more moments when you feel HP or LP. So as you work on building healthy habits in this chapter, try to introduce new behaviors, or ones you temporarily retired, into your life in a consistent manner to optimize your ability to think clearly and have the physical and emotional energy to tackle your valued life goals.

Larks and Owls

We all have circadian clocks, but you may have noticed that yours is set to be either an early riser—a *lark* or to be a night person—an *owl*. If you are a lark, you perform your best in the morning and so go to sleep on the early side. If you are an owl, you prefer to sleep in, perform your best later in the day, and prefer to go to bed pretty late. Lark or owl, you will serve yourself well to choose consistent times for your routines that also match the hours when your body is hitting that groove. For example, my family comes from a long line of night owls. Despite sporadic phases of morning exercise, I don't think a single one of us has ever successfully built an exercise habit before work. But when I call a family member at 9 p.m., I'm never surprised to hear the whir of a treadmill in the background. In stark contrast, my husband and his family go to swim or Jazzercise at wee hours of the morning that feel like nighttime to me.

Keep this basic preference in mind as you read the following sections and think about forming your own healthy habits. It's always best to honor your unique circadian tendencies because that will better set you up for success.

How to Establish New Habits

There is no doubt that on a typical day you will function better if you have your basic life domains in balance, which includes sleep, exercise, eating, substances, and relaxation. But you're also busy and strapped for time. I get it. Given this reality, I draw from research on habit formation to offer ways in which these self-care behaviors can form the backbone of your day-to-day life.

A habit is a repeated behavior that is set off by routine cues in your environment. A behavior turns into a habit when it follows the same cue every time, especially a circadian one. It also needs to be immediately reinforcing, for example the behavior makes you feel good, gives you something you want, or removes something you don't want. Over time, the decision-making about the behavior—and the behavior itself—become automatic.

The challenging part is establishing the habit, which is what this chapter will help you do. Because trying to establish new habits across multiple domains would feel overwhelming, I encourage you to pick just one. With your first habit area in motion—often referred to as a *keystone habit*[3]—other behaviors that are related tend to cascade into place. In other words, the first habit can have a domino effect. For example, your keystone habit of going to sleep at the same time every night increases the chance you'll be able to roll out of bed when your alarm goes off. This can foster additional healthy habits, because you will have enough time to exercise (since you didn't hit snooze), which increases the chance that you will crave a healthy lunch. As you read, try to identify what your keystone habit is so that it can naturally affect the other domains.

In the following sections, I teach you to establish routine cues in your environment that set the stage for developing self-care habits. I suggest that you read the whole chapter and, while reading, think about which domain you want to focus on as your keystone habit. Next, after you have picked your keystone habit, go back and reread that section to prepare for implementing the targeted strategies. As you begin to practice your keystone habit, track how often you engage in your target behavior and what happens when you do. To track easily and effectively, you can use the sample monitoring form offered later in the chapter. Tracking your routines will help you refine your efforts and make continued progress as the weeks progress.

To help you build these habits, in each section I first provide healthy guidelines to help you get the lay of the land. After that, you will find suggestions for establishing specific cues to initiate and integrate the habit into your life in ways that support both larks and owls.

Healthy Sleep Habits

If your sleep schedule is all over the place, consider making sleep your keystone habit. As you already learned, consistent sleep patterns positively influence daily secretion of cortisol and melatonin, which can promote healthy levels of energy, alertness, and appetite. In contrast, inconsistent sleep patterns can make you vulnerable as you suffer the consequences of changes in energy, appetite, and possibly mood. Additionally, if you're flat-out sleep deprived, you know firsthand that you don't function as well and you probably don't shoot the straightest arrows. There is ample data that shows poor or problematic sleep has negative effects on effort, mood, and cognitive capacities.

General Sleep Guidelines

Sleep Times: It's best to have routine sleeping and waking times, even during the weekend, plus or minus one hour. A good way to make a permanent change to your sleep times is to work in fifteen-minute intervals. Let's say you are currently going to bed at 12 a.m. and you continuously wake feeling exhausted when your alarm sounds at 6:30 a.m. Sleeping later is not an option. In that case, you may realize you could get more of the sleep you need by going to bed at 11 p.m. As you make this transition, set your time for falling asleep to 11:45 p.m., then after a few nights shift it another fifteen minutes to 11:30 p.m., and so on.

Duration: The idea that we need eight hours of sleep has been worked into our psyches. But it's not a magical number—there is actually a lot of variability. Go with what works for your body. If you're not sure, you can monitor how you feel during the day. How sleepy are you? Are you too drowsy to concentrate? Are you especially irritable? These may be signs that you need more sleep. It's true that sleeping too much can also contribute to daytime fatigue, so be mindful of oversleeping.

Naps: When you nap for longer than thirty minutes, you will feel less "hungry" for sleep at night. Long naps can mess up your routine, as they lead to falling asleep later, which might make you feel overtired in the morning or even oversleep—and so the cycle continues. Some people do nap without any problems, so learn about your own body. Generally speaking, naps lasting longer than thirty minutes might not be helpful.

What You Consume: When you drink alcohol or eat a heavy meal right before bed, you may fall asleep without a problem but have poor sleep quality.

Bedroom Environment: Make your bedroom feel comfortable and as close to a personal sanctuary as you can. This includes the temperature of the room, which might need to be negotiated if your bed partner has a different preference. Other features might be sounds from a white-noise machine, a comfortable mattress, pillows stuffed just right, the heaviness of a blanket, or a small amount of light. Earplugs and an eye mask are excellent accessories if you prefer to block out sensory input while sleeping.

When You Can't Fall Asleep: Staying in bed and trying to fall asleep for a long period of time is not effective. If you can't sleep and you've been laying there for thirty minutes, it is typically better to get up and do something relaxing out of bed like stretching, reading, or folding laundry. Return to the bed when you think you will be able to nod off.

Worries and Thoughts: If you tend to worry or you can't turn off your mind at bedtime, and it keeps you awake, here are some preventative measures you can do earlier in the day.

- Take time to get your thoughts out well before bedtime. Write them down, speak them into a recording app on your phone, or talk about them with a trusted friend or loved one. Making time for the thoughts to be expressed will help keep them from creeping in when it's time to relax.

- Do relaxation exercises, such as the progressive muscle relaxation offered in the next section. Or you could do one of the exercises suggested in Principle 3 to help you cope with strong emotions.

- Consider making exercise your keystone habit and see if that helps reduce your mental activity at night.

Avoiding Life by Going to Bed: Sometimes it's tempting to get into bed because you feel sad, lonely, or you want to escape life. This applies to going to bed early and sneaking in a daytime nap. Sleeping can be a way to avoid the pain of being awake, which feels good in the moment but also prevents you from engaging in things you value, working toward important goals, and encountering other sources of pleasure. Moreover, while it feels soothing in the moment, it can continue to exacerbate sleep irregularities. Crawling into bed does more harm than good. So gently and lovingly try to stay awake. Principle 3 will help you learn skills to break avoidance traps such as this classic one.

Cues to Wind Down and Become Sleepy

The first step is creating cues to tell your body that it is time to wind down. This prebedtime ritual, also referred to as a "buffer zone," takes place roughly an hour before bed and is the transitional time when you give your mind and body permission to become less alert and *slow down*. First, choose a time when you will regularly fall asleep. As a lark, this might be 10 p.m., whereas for an owl it may be closer to 11:30 p.m. or midnight. Then, the cue for the buffer zone will come about forty-five to sixty minutes before this.

This may be easy for larks, who naturally get sleepy at night. In that case, the cue to wind down will often be internal as you notice initial signs of sleepiness around 9 p.m. On the other hand, owls might need to set an intentional cue such as an alarm, the end of a favorite show, or your lark of a partner heading to bed, to help you know it's time to make the transition around 10:30 p.m.

Activities in the buffer zone are designed to help you relax. They can include getting ready for bed by putting on pajamas and brushing your teeth, which might be followed by something relaxing such as practicing a guided meditation, listening to music, reading, or watching TV for a limited period of time. If you tend to toss and turn and struggle with quantity or quality of sleep, then it is best to wind down out of bed and, ideally, outside the bedroom. Reserving the bed exclusively for sleeping will help cue your body that it is time to *sleep* when you get into the bed.

Cues to Close Your Eyes and Fall Asleep

If you're a lark, the cues to sleep may be as simple as getting into bed and turning off the light. If your buffer zone activity has you already in bed, maybe the signals that it is time to sleep are setting your alarm for the next morning, turning off the light, and assuming your regular position in bed. If you have a bed partner who goes to sleep at the same time, maybe you say goodnight to each other. (And if you have a bed partner who goes to sleep after you, hopefully they are skilled at crawling in later without waking you up.) Then off you go to sleep.

For owls, sleepiness can feel elusive at times. The repetition of waking up at the same time and winding down at the same time every day will teach your body that when the wind-down routine comes to a close, it is time for sleep. That said, there may be nights when a relaxing hour has passed and you *still* feel awake. In those moments, what do you do? You don't want to fret about it because the more anxious you get, the harder it will be to fall asleep. Instead, you might want to build in additional external cues to help communicate to your body that it is time to sleep.

These additional cues can include a five-minute relaxation exercise that you do in bed, with the light off, right before you assume a sleeping position. You might take slow, diaphragmatic breaths for a few minutes (I'll share detailed instructions for this in Principle 4), or you could evoke a visual image of yourself in a peaceful place and imagine all the sights, sounds, and smells around you. You might say a prayer. When sleep feels far from me, I do an abbreviated version of *progressive muscle relaxation,* or PMR. PMR involves intentionally tightening and then relaxing different muscle groups to elicit a relaxation response. You can work through multiple muscle groups across the body—legs, feet, hands, arms, shoulders, stomach, face—tightening each area for 5 to 10 seconds before loosening and releasing. In my abridged version, I squeeze my hands into fists, then loosen and open them, noticing the contrasting sensations from tight to relaxed. Next, I clench my toes for a few seconds, then loosen them, again noticing the contrasting sensations from tight to relaxed. Because I have repeated this simple sequence so often right before falling asleep, the act has become, over time, a powerful cue that it's time to sleep.

Experiment and see what happens. Do note that repetition is the key to making any of these suggestions work. The more you get yourself wound down in the same way, tucked in at the same time, and out of bed at the same time, the easier it will be for your body to fall asleep when you turn off the lights and close your eyes.

Cues to Wake, Get Out of Bed, and Become Alert

It's just as important to set a routine wake-up time and to keep this pretty consistent throughout all seven days of the week, ideally within the hour. Most of us wake to an alarm. For larks, it may be easier to skip hitting the snooze button and hop right out of bed. Perhaps opening the blinds, making your bed, or showering cues you to become alert. You could also set up your morning so that waking up is a cue to put on your exercise clothes and head right to the treadmill, as morning is a great time for larks to fit this in. So your cues might begin with the alarm, which leads to grabbing your exercise clothes and putting on your sneakers. Then off you go to exercise.

For the owls, the phrase "difficulty getting out of bed" may ring true. Just remember, the pain is temporary. Sleeping in, and even sleeping too much, can be tempting but will create more stress once you finally get out of bed. There goes time to make breakfast. It could be tempting to drive a little too fast in your rush to get to work on time. Woops! If you want to set yourself up for success with the cognitive, emotional, and physical energy to meet your goals, I strongly encourage you to make it a top priority and point of initial focus to get up at your set time without majorly snoozing—plus or minus one hour. You might resist: "What? You want me to be rested, but you're telling me to wake up early, like, all the time?" While your preference may be to sleep until 9 or 10 a.m. or later, remember that the more consistently you go to sleep and wake up at the same times, the easier it'll be for your body to get going when the alarm buzzes. Waking at 7:30 a.m. might start to feel just a touch easier if you were able to get yourself to sleep at 11:30 p.m. the night before.

But it's still hard. Here are some additional strategies to help you get out of bed on time.

Alarms: Use multiple alarm clocks that…wait for it…are out of reach when you are in bed, set to staggered times. Why? You know exactly why. You are addicted to hitting the snooze button. You can also download phone apps that make you solve math problems before the alarm will turn off. That way, you can't hit snooze and not remember doing so. And waking up to an energizing music playlist, rather than the dreaded "Beep… Beep…Beep" sound, can change the tone of waking up from dread-filled to inspirational or playful.

Stretches: Do some gentle stretching in bed. For example, you can do a soft side stretch. To do this, sit up in bed with your legs crossed. Interlace your fingers with palms facing out and extend both arms straight above your head. Slowly bend from the waist, first to one side, then return to center, and then to the other side. If you are familiar with yoga, try going into Child's Pose and cleansing yourself with some deep *ujjayi* breaths.

Motivations: Find things that motivate you to get up. I am always hungry when I wake up, so the thought of breakfast is what typically lures me out of bed. Needing to use the bathroom is motivating, so consider the surprising value of mild discomfort from drinking a bedtime tea the night before. Getting out of bed could give you more time with family. It could mean you have time to call a friend or loved one before he or she heads to work for the day. Any of these may be all the enticement you need—just remind yourself of it when you're debating whether or not to hit snooze.

Ask for Help: You may want to ask for help from trusted people in your world. Young children wanting or needing help with their own morning rituals are sometimes all the assistance you need, since you're already accountable to them. Alternatively, you could ask someone to soothe your transition, perhaps by having them call or have sent an encouraging email or text message the night before that you read upon awakening. I like to call my lark of a husband, who is always up before me, into the room when my alarm goes off. He has me sit up in bed, which can feel painful, and then he hugs me—a reward that softens the blow of sitting upright.

Activities: Opening the blinds is a small but major step you can take. The bright light exposure, weather and season dependent, strengthens your circadian clock. I also highly recommend making your bed so that you're less likely to nap later or crawl right back in. You'll also feel accomplished by seeing how nice the room looks with this little bit of order you created—a special note of thanks to the Veterans who taught this lesson to me. Taking a shower is an easy lure when you say to yourself, "All I have to do is go and stand under hot water, which feels wonderful. That's all I need to do." We are so fortunate that most of us have access to hot water. Don't destroy our planet by showering for hours, but do luxuriate in the soothing power of warm water as you transition into your day.

Coffee or Tea Rituals: Create a morning ritual of coffee or tea in its special, reserved mug. The few moments when you breathe in the smell of the coffee or tea might cue an opportunity to tell yourself what you're looking forward to, or to recall a goal you want to focus on achieving that day. The small acts of taking out your special mug, using your senses to increase your alertness, and triggering enthusiasm for the coming day are excellent ways to communicate to your body that it is time to get going, increase your cognitive activity, and prepare to show up for what matters.

Have you noticed one theme in all these suggestions? They help you make your morning routine enjoyable, or as enjoyable as is possible within your circadian style. The question to ask yourself is: What can you do to soothe your way into the day? Because rewarding life experiences are just waiting for you to show up for them.

As these suggestions show, larks and owls alike can establish cues that communicate to their bodies when it is time to get sleepy, time to fall asleep, and time to wake up. The biggest challenge for larks is staying awake before it's time to sleep. And owls may struggle most with falling asleep at a prescribed bedtime and getting up at a prescribed wake-up time. Stabilizing the sleeping and waking pattern through repetition will help your body operate in a balanced manner, which contributes so much to your overall feelings of well-being.

Healthy Exercise Habits

Intellectually, you may know how good exercising is for you. Exercise helps with weight management, cardiovascular health, diabetes, bone density, cancer risk, fall risk, and longevity—to name a few. Exercise is widely recommended as an add-on to standard depression treatment and, for a patient who isn't ready to seek treatment, as a first step to initiate on his or her own. Why? Exercise increases your self-efficacy, which is the belief that you are an effective human being. It improves mood and leads to neural changes that increase feelings of well-being, such as more endorphins and blood circulation, as well as reduced levels of the stress hormone cortisol. In short, exercise is an essential part of optimal daily life.

What can you notice when you do versus don't exercise? Do you carry certain tension or aches in parts of your body when you don't? Do you feel more confident or relaxed when you do? Does exercise fit into any of your top values related to physical health, emotional well-being, or self-care?

General Exercise Guidelines

To illustrate many of the suggestions, I'd like to introduce Craig. Like all of us, he benefits from exercise and, like most of us, struggles to turn his plans to exercise into actual activity. Craig feels tired after work, he struggles with the thought *I just don't care,* and when he does get to the gym for cardio or a weight circuit he is self-conscious and it feels like torture 75 percent of the time. As I provide suggestions for how to personalize exercise to fit Craig's needs and preferences, see if any of them might work for you.

Make Exercise Social: Doing activities with others can make them more enjoyable as you talk, share tips, and encourage each other. Also, knowing that others are counting on you to show up may make you accountable. Craig might plan a walk or bike ride with a friend. He might take a group class or work privately with a trainer.

Hold Yourself Accountable: Despite the best-laid plans, it can feel easy to simply change your mind. Craig can say he wants to go for a walk in his neighborhood, but when 6 p.m. arrives he may think of other things he can and should be doing that feel easier. He needs a way to hold himself accountable, which will increase his commitment and the chance exercising will happen.

One accountability strategy is to socially commit to following through on his exercise plan. For example, if Craig is emailing a friend or talking to a work colleague about his evening, he can tell them he has a 6:30 p.m. exercise class. It might seem minor, but the act of saying or writing it—even if he knows they're not going to ask about the class tomorrow—helps him feel like he really wants to be the kind of person who follows through.

Craig could make himself accountable financially. Signing up for fitness classes ahead of time helps because he will be financially penalized if he doesn't show up. Alternatively, he could put a dollar or two in a container every time he *does* go so that after a certain number of times he'll have enough money to treat himself to something he enjoys. This treat would be a celebration of Craig's hard work, which can feel motivating and increase his accountability.

Find Your Niche: Craig tends to get lost in his thoughts when he exercises alone, which puts him in a very HN state. But he discovered that when he plays basketball, he feels like a carefree kid. To develop and strengthen your exercise habit, find activities that suit you. Remember, "exercise" is an open term. I always struggle with distance running and want to cry during classes that are styled after boot camp. But I enjoy more meditative exercise, so I look forward to Pilates and yoga. Don't do the exercise you think you should do—find the exercise that matches your style. Here are some additional suggestions, which are among many options.

- Capture the flag

- Climbing the stairs in your apartment or office building

- Dance classes

- High-intensity training

- Kickball

- Online routines offered for free on YouTube

- Rock climbing in an indoor studio or outdoors

- Tennis

- Walking around the shopping mall

- Walking in nature

- Water aerobics

- Wii Fit games

Pick Something Convenient: If Craig gets into a groove of playing pickup basketball games but then has a three-month stretch when he needs to work extra late for a big project, what then? He could buy a used stationary bike online and hop on for forty-five minutes while watching his favorite TV show. The trick would be for Craig to make it convenient. A stationary bike eliminates the travel time to and from the gym, and he can flex start times as well as how long he stays on the bike. He can increase his heart rate without feeling miserable running, and an indoor bike is not influenced by weather or nighttime. Also, the TV show keeps Craig from getting stuck in his head, as tends to happen when he's exercising without distraction.

In other words, fit exercise in where, when, and however you can. Also, exercise can be spread across your day for five minutes here, ten minutes there. Try searching "five-minute workout" on YouTube or go to the *New York Times* article titled

"Really, Really Short Workouts" for inspiration on brief, high-intensity workouts.[4]

Set Minimum and Maximum Goals: Craig gets overwhelmed when he sets exercise goals high because he feels too intimidated to even begin a session. With a reasonable minimum goal, like riding the stationary bike for ten minutes, anything after that is icing on the cake (or, um, olive oil on the salad). The Zeigarnik effect is a social psychology phenomenon that you can use in your favor, as it relies on the observation that we feel a lot more tension when we don't complete things we start. So if you can talk yourself into starting an exercise session because reaching your minimum goal isn't too overwhelming, then you might actually find that you want to keep going and surpass your minimum. Craig might find himself saying, "I set a ten-minute goal, but I really want to reach that next mile marker…" and off he goes. But when he doesn't, it's totally okay, as he is still strengthening the habit of showing up for exercise when planned and associating exercise with feelings of accomplishment.

It's also good to set maximum goals. Sometimes, when Craig really gets going, he can overdo his workouts. This can create problems, as he might, at worst, injure his body and, at the least, make it psychologically harder to show up for exercise the next day. He may say to himself, "Oh man, I don't have the energy to do *that* again!" So maximum goals are helpful to keep you going for the long haul, whether you set a time, distance, or repetition limit.

Putting it together, you might get on the treadmill, being satisfied with yourself if you jog for only ten minutes. If you want to keep going that's fine, but you can't exceed thirty minutes. In other words, make the task less overwhelming with a minimum goal—which can increase over time as your habit and body strengthen. And don't let yourself make the task herculean—though this maximum goal will also increase over time as your body strengthens and you learn how much pushing is reasonable. Better to take your time building up the muscle of exercising, mentally and physically, so that you don't burn out.

Log Your Goals and Accomplishments: Keeping track of his exercise in a log promotes a tremendous sense of accomplishment for Craig. It's no wonder wireless activity trackers like Fitbit have been such a hit; they offer user-friendly ways to engage goals and quantify progress over time. Online communities help keep engagement with these goals ongoing, fresh, and interactive. Some workplaces hold challenges and competitions to encourage employee wellness.

Make it a challenge for yourself to log your goals, privately or publicly. Do whatever keeps you on your toes (literally!) and feeling great. When you see progress before your very eyes, that's great, and when you have people to celebrate it with you, that's even better. If you have a naturally competitive nature, use that to your benefit and participate in community forums where you can best your comrades.

Protect Your Exercise Time: When you are invited to do things at times that conflict with your exercise schedule, you'll have to evaluate them on a case-by-case basis. But do be willing to stick to your guns a bit. Craig loves his Thursday night basketball game, but say a friend invites him to meet up for dinner and drinks after work. What should he do in this approach-approach conflict? If this is a friend visiting from out of town—and he can't cajole the friend to work out—sure, this may be a good time to be flexible. But if the friend is someone he sees frequently, he could request that they meet at a coffee shop beforehand or for a light bite after the game is over. Protecting your exercise time becomes even more pertinent if you identified that physical or emotional health is a top value for the next 6 to 12 months. Consider ways to engage in both opportunities and, if that cannot be reconciled, consider prioritizing your health. And yes, along the way, something may have to give. Let's just say that if you are able to squeeze in exercise followed by dinner plans, there is a chance you might not be able to squeeze in a shower as well. Just hope you're with someone who has a weak sense of smell!

Cues to Exercise

When establishing an exercise habit—especially if you struggle with it at first—it's best to match your efforts with the times when you're in peak mode to perform. Are you better off exercising in the morning or night?

If you're considering setting a morning workout, do note: a crucial determinant in successfully waking up and working out is whether you went to bed at a reasonable hour. If your sleep habits are off-kilter and you've been going to bed later than your norm, you may need to make sleep your keystone habit. Clearing up your sleep will naturally influence your ability to wake up in the morning and exercise. But if you are going to bed later than usual because you are awake worrying or feeling too keyed up to sleep, exercise might be the keystone habit that cascades into feeling tired at night, which will improve your sleep.

For larks who do better early in the day, a morning workout might help establish an exercise habit. Your wake-up ritual might follow this order: get out of bed, make your bed, open the blinds, change into workout clothes, head into the kitchen for water and a snack, and then head to wherever you go for exercise, be it the gym, your at-home treadmill, or your yoga mat in the living room. Maybe to pep up this routine you read an inspiring quote of the day or something spiritual that energizes you right before you get dressed. Maybe you create a "wake up and get moving" playlist that you listen to while suiting up in your exercise clothes. Some people even sleep in their gym clothes—they're comfortable and the process of getting ready becomes automatic when they are already geared up for success.

For owls, if it makes sense to exercise in the morning, try it. Then gauge how successful you are. You may or may not struggle to establish this new habit. If you find yourself scheduling an early morning workout, hitting snooze, saying "I'll do better tomorrow," and then tomorrow comes and you do the same thing—don't be hard on yourself. Owls are notorious for hitting the snooze button through a planned morning run. If this happens, match your goal with the time you are in peak mode to perform and work out in the afternoon or evening. Those times may feel a little more natural.

Your exercise ritual may begin after work when you walk in the door to your home, which is your cue to change into workout clothes and head to the spot where you exercise. If you get too tempted by the sight of your couch, you could head straight from work to your exercise facility. When you pair leaving your workplace with going to exercise, you establish a powerful cue, particularly because going home instead would be a big deviation from your habit. You can streamline the process of going from point A to point B by packing your workout clothes in the morning so you have them with you already. This step further cuts down on the many temptations of home (including Netflix). Finally, exercising immediately after your workday ends can set a cue for you to relax and leave those work-related thoughts and stresses behind at work. Indeed, exercising may function as a reward for a long day at work—imagine that!

One crucial aspect of successfully working out in the evening is planning your meals so that you are not uncomfortably hungry when it's time to exercise. When you're feeling ravenous, getting yourself to workout enjoyably will be much harder to achieve. If your meal schedules are off and are keeping you from having the energy to exercise, you may want to make eating your keystone habit. Or maybe you tend to forget to prepare your meals, or get too busy to eat at all, because you have not worked out and don't feel hungry enough. In this case, exercise might be the keystone habit that naturally triggers cues to plan balanced meals or to stop at the grocery store on the way home.

For both larks and owls, whatever your cues are, the main trick is to make them so consistent in your environment that the routine becomes automatic. To further increase the likelihood that you create an exercise habit, you may want to set up an initial reward for yourself. Maybe that means recording it in a log, which feels good when you track progress. Perhaps you celebrate your success with others, as I'll discuss more in Principle 5. Or you could treat yourself in a reasonable way, like picking up a caffè Americano on the way to work or allowing yourself to watch a second episode of your favorite TV show when you get home. Natural rewards might include the endorphin release, sense of accomplishment, and feelings of contentment that can be enough to motivate you. The more rewarding exercise feels, the more likely it is to shape into a habit, so be sure to give yourself credit that you did it.

Healthy Eating Habits

To reduce the feeling that your life is a giant bucket of stress, consider your fuel sources. How do you feel throughout the day? Lethargic? Headachy? Irritable? As already discussed, problematic sleep could be a culprit, and here I want to focus on food, since what you are eating could also be a contributing factor. As I'll discuss more in Principle 3, lethargy, headaches, and irritability are types of triggering events that increase your potential to procrastinate—especially when a goal activity requires a high amount of effort. When you don't feel well, you are more likely to say "I'll do it when I feel better," and to give up and give in, even though action is optimal in that very moment. Eating well *for your body* can set you up to be just a little more nourished, a little more energized, and a little more physically and emotionally able to tackle day-to-day challenges.

In case you don't already know it, what you eat matters on all levels. The things that go in your body have incredible implications for your health and feelings of well-being. Eating is a major lifestyle factor that influences many medical conditions including the two biggies: heart disease and diabetes. Lifestyle is the best way to prevent these conditions, even when genetic predisposition is a factor. Diet also determines the composition of your gut microbiome, which increases or reduces long-term risks for developing conditions like colon cancer, Crohn's disease, diabetes, obesity, and rheumatoid arthritis—to name just a few.

It can be helpful to find out more about your body's specific needs. If you suspect that you might be shooting yourself in the gut, so to speak, and want clarity on how or why, I recommend meeting with a gastroenterologist, allergist, or nutritionist. They can perform tests to see what food allergies you may have and identify whether or not your diet is providing you with the right types of nutrients for your lifestyle. For example, if you are vegan or if you are exposed to very little sunlight, are you getting all the nutrients you need? Specialists can teach you how to figure out what foods impact you adversely by eliminating potentially aggravating foods for a brief period of time and then reintroducing them, one by one.

In addition to identifying what foods are healthy for your body, which might involve consulting a specialist, other crucial components are to create healthy behaviors around eating and to establish routine cues for habitual meal preparation and mealtime.

General Eating Guidelines

The Kitchen: Just as your bed is a cue for sleep, your kitchen is a cue for eating. If you fill your kitchen with foods that are relatively healthy for you and your family, the kitchen will become associated with healthy eating. Try to eat only in the dining areas and not in other rooms throughout your house. Your couch can be associated with relaxing or family bonding, but try not to associate it with eating. The risk is that you fall prey to a cue to eat when it's not mealtime or you're not hungry. And see if you can avoid working at the kitchen table, as you may feel inclined to snack as you do it.

Hunger: Ask yourself, "Am I really hungry?" If you are craving something and it's not your planned time to eat, let fifteen minutes pass. No matter how hungry you think you are, see if you can wait fifteen minutes. Then evaluate it: "Am I still legitimately hungry?" If so, go for an easy-to-grab food that will nourish rather than deplete you.

Pay Attention to Eating: Savor flavorful and tasty food! Turn off the TV. Quit multitasking. Take a break from a stressful conversation. Think about it: you're not eating constantly, so it's a joy and a luxury when you do, and it can function as a reward. Strawberries, avocado, homemade nut butter…what delicacies. Become a hedonist by paying attention to the richness of the flavors in foods that give you energy. Sitting down at the kitchen table or in the dining room helps you do this, because it reduces distractions and cues you to be in the moment with your meal.

Introduce Variety: Focus on foods to add rather than foods to eliminate. What type of variety do you want to introduce? Test out new foods. I just discovered kohlrabi, which is a wonderful type of cabbage. Also, you might not believe it, but roasted parsnips are really tasty. Find a healthy food blog that inspires you. I owe a huge load of thanks to the blog "Chocolate Covered Katie," which offers healthy deserts and easy meals that rely on some of my favorite ingredients: rolled oats, nut butters, and bananas.

Cut Down on Temptations: That said, if an unhealthy food is not in your house, you can't grab it from the cabinet during a weak moment. So even if you're not overly focused on what to eliminate, you can also resist temptation by turning certain foods, like ice cream or donuts, into special foods that you thoughtfully plan to enjoy outside the house. Plus, out of sight is out of mind, so there are some foods you might not remember to crave without the visual trigger of seeing it on your shelf.

If you work in an office, temptation will likely be constant. There are candy bowls, birthday cakes, breakfast meeting bagels, and other types of extra food lying around. If you bring food with you to work that you actually enjoy, you'll experience less desire to eat the extra food. You can leave the room, bring your own food into the meeting, or sip on a hot beverage. If others push you—"Don't you want a piece?"—practice getting comfortable saying no. A simple "I'm good, no thank you" or "I already brought my breakfast" or "I just ate my lunch, thanks" can often suffice.

Cook Conveniently: Remember that cooking doesn't have to mean following a recipe or even using the stove. A crockpot, microwave, or toaster oven can do a lot. Take the foods and combinations of ingredients you really like and repeat them, relying on go-to ingredients regularly. You don't have to be repeatedly original—the priority is simply to eat balanced meals at routine times.

Snacking On the Go: Channel your inner grandmother and bring food with you. Anticipate that 3.5 hours from now you will likely feel hungry. When you are out and about, your options are not cheap, and it can be harder to make healthy choices. Bring an apple and almonds in the car or in your bag. You can even tally up the money you save this way and put it toward something special.

Avoid an Eating Spiral: Try not to fall into the classic trap: "I ate something I shouldn't have, now it's a bad day, so I might as well binge since I already strayed." You'll be tempted to be more restrictive the next day, which starts the yo-yo of being "good," followed by being "bad," followed by being "good" again. At best this is problematic eating, at worst you start to get yourself into disordered eating habits. Best advice? Resume your normal eating habits right away, because one aberrant data point won't destroy you. You ate birthday cake at work when you weren't planning for it? *C'est la vie.* Revert to your regularly scheduled eating plans and try to learn from the experience. If you don't want to fall prey to cake the next time you're tempted, what will help you resist?

Automatic Prompts to Eat: Notice what prompts you to change your eating. Is it thoughts of body dissatisfaction like "I'm too fat, I better not eat that"? Or is it satisfaction, as in "I earned that with my good performance review"? Do your habits change when you're tired, stressed, sad, anxious, or bored? If so, you'll find more discussion about coping with emotions in ways that don't take you further from your goals in Principle 3.

Food Monitoring: Whether you use comfort food to cope with tough moments or you eat without paying attention, if you are having a difficult time with the quantity or type of food that you put in your body, monitor it. Simply write down what you're eating, the quantity you're eating, and when you're eating it—which can be as simple as noting that it's breakfast, lunch, dinner, or a snack. You can adapt the tracking form offered at the end of this chapter to write down what you're eating. There are websites where you can log for free. Excel spreadsheets work great and so does writing it down in a notebook or journal.

Monitoring is one of the best strategies for changing behavior. When you're keeping track, you don't want to see certain behaviors go into your log. Owning up to them can be challenging, so be gentle as well as honest with yourself. See what insights you gain. You will likely start to notice patterns: Maybe there is a particular time of day when you are vulnerable to sneaking in a bite. Perhaps when you're stressed you make an impulsive stop for fast food on the way home from work. If you buy ice cream for the kids at the supermarket, do you eat it all that night while watching TV? What patterns can you find?

Cues to Nourish Your Body with Healthy Food

It's easy to confuse actual hunger with psychological hunger. Internal cues signaling actual hunger can include sensing an empty stomach, hearing your belly growl, feeling lightheaded, or experiencing a drop in energy. If you can rely on your awareness of bodily cues, then these cues may be sufficient. Unfortunately, it's really easy to confuse types of hunger. Psychological hunger is the state of wanting to eat because it's rewarding—all else ceases to matter for those delicious seconds. Basically, you're craving a spike of dopamine from your pleasure center. You want to eat because it's rewarding, comforting, and pleasurable.

Most of us do experience confusion between actual and psychological hunger, and we eat when we're stressed or sad or mad or bored. These are not helpful cues for when to eat. For those who struggle, helpful routine cues can result from eating planned meals at *predictable* times of day. Here's a sample day that uses context and time to establish a predictable eating routine.

Meal 1: Wake up at 6:30 a.m., get dressed, go into the kitchen at 7:00 a.m. (cue): eat breakfast

Snack 1: At work, after your regular 9 to 10 a.m. meeting finishes (cue): eat a light snack

Meal 2: At work, the clock or an alarm you set strikes 1 p.m. (cue): eat lunch

Snack 2: At work, you notice energy falling (internal cue) or clock strikes 4 p.m. (external cue): eat snack

Meal 3: Return home, change into comfortable clothes, go into the kitchen, open the fridge (cue): prep and eat dinner

This demonstrates how you can make sure your meals occur at predictable times. Doing so will prevent overeating because a schedule like this has no room for munching in between your planned meals and snacks, which occur every 3 to 4 hours. This will also help if you struggle to eat enough and will stave off the "Woops! I forgot to eat" and the "I'm so stressed I lost my appetite" moments. With a routine, your body gets ready to eat at these regular times.

Being able to successfully follow a daily meal routine does require you to also have a habit in place for doing the necessary food prep work. Then your food is ready for you, and you can eat on cue. Though at times you'll eat out or order in, generally the best way to eat foods that nourish your unique needs involves prepping meals in your own kitchen ahead of mealtime.

Cues to Prepare Meals Ahead of Time

The first step of meal prep is having your ingredients on hand before you feel hungry. I highly recommend a routine of going food shopping for kitchen staples and special ingredients you will need for the next few days. Because if eating a meal is predicated on first buying the groceries, you're already hungry when you go to the market so will grab whatever is available— which won't be the healthiest choice. Or you'll order in or go out to eat instead. When you buy what you need in advance, it will be just a touch easier to prepare it when scheduled and then eat it at the planned time. If you shop for food in the European style and are in the habit of picking up just a few ingredients each day, you can still routinely stop at the store before your hunger floodgates open. The goal is to plan and buy what you'll need *before you are hungry.* Then you can sched-ule routine times to prepare those ingredients.

Making Food Prep Enjoyable

Food prep? Are you someone who would rather pass on it and put something premade in the microwave? Regardless of how it gets done, what is important is that you are prepared to eat balanced meals on a schedule. Here are some suggestions you can experiment with to see if food prep can become more enjoyable.

- Pair food preparation with something you enjoy— like listening to music, NPR, or a podcast you love—as you chop and simmer.

- Begin preheating the oven before your favorite show. During a commercial break or a pause at the ten-minute mark, put whatever you're preparing— fish, chicken, veggies, potatoes—in the oven. Then keep it cooking while your show continues.

- Make it a social activity and invite someone to join you.

- Try a meal delivery service that sends fresh ingredients to your door. This can streamline your time, as it eliminates the need for going to the grocery store with an itemized list—which is time consuming when you use recipes.

- Keep it simple, and create a personal challenge, by limiting the number of ingredients you use per dish.

- Chop your vegetables after you get home from the market, before you pop them in the refrigerator. This will help you when you get hungry and just want to reach for something. Also, you can easily throw a handful into a plastic container to bring with you on the go.

- Cook up a storm once a month and freeze individual meals that you can pop in the microwave or in the oven when you're ready for them.

- If you really, truly hate food prep, see if you can negotiate so that someone else in your household does the dirty work. Life is short, right?

Timing Your Food Prep

When can you devote time to prepping meals? I encourage you to set routine times in your week or day so that you are all set. Here are a variety of styles to choose from, so you can find times that work best for you. Whenever you choose, do it consistently, in ways that work with your level of energy at that time of day.

- Some people do a lot of cooking during the weekend, and then have their meals ready for the week. Weekdays can simply be too chaotic, so food prep becomes a relaxing routine for weekends.

- Other people cook dinner every evening as a form of relaxation, and then the next day they bring left-overs to work for lunch.

- Larks might enjoy waking up early to prep food in the morning.

- Alternatively, making food at night, including tomorrow's lunch, might help larks stay awake until their scheduled bedtime. For example, evening cues might be: put on pajamas, turn on soothing music, enter the kitchen, make tea, start prepping tomorrow's meals.

- Owls with energy at night might enjoy preparing tomorrow's lunch after dinner, so they can be in a better position to streamline their mornings (and maximize sleep time).

- Alternatively, making food in the morning may help owls transition into the day. For example, morning cues might be: enter the kitchen, make coffee, start prepping for lunch as you slowly become more alert.

Try out different options and see what works best for you. Whenever you choose, choose consistently, and work with your level of energy. Overall, the way to establish healthy eating habits is to follow these four tips:

- Have the necessary ingredients in the house and buy ingredients that nourish you

- Follow a routine time to prepare your meals

- Make meal preparation enjoyable

- Eat your meals at set times of day

Healthy Habits for Watching Your Substances

In addition to sleeping, exercising, and eating, another crucial aspect of self-care is paying attention to what substances, in general, you put into your body. I have already discussed food choices, so in this section I'll focus on vitamins, medications, recreational drugs, cigarette smoking, and drinking. The path to optimize your daily functioning, so that you feel up to making the effort to engage in other rewarding activities, includes taking your vitamins and medications in a stable and regimented manner, and limiting drugs, cigarettes, and alcohol. First I'll focus on suggestions for cues to remember to take your medication, and after I'll address why I want you to consider sobriety as you work through this book.

Regularity with Meds

It's important to take vitamins and medications as recommended, at routine times of day. Inconsistently taking vitamins and medicine, which I'll refer to with the catch-all term "medication," can have physical, cognitive, and emotional side effects—and may even be dangerous. Most medication is meant to be taken at the same time each day, at routine intervals such as every 12 hours. Timing may also be based on when you eat, as the medication might work best with or without an empty stomach and some may cause you to feel ill otherwise.

Some people are reluctant or ambivalent about their medication because they don't want to have to be on it for the rest of their lives or they don't fully agree with the doctor's recommendation. It is good to be a critical thinker, and it is good to advocate for yourself. But taking medication inconsistently is likely not helping you. If you want to evaluate the consequences of taking it to see if you want to continue with the medication, then you need to collect data to share with your doctor. I encourage you to take it consistently, write down notes on what happens when you do, and then use that information to collaborate and problem-solve with your health-care provider to refine your medication strategy. You can use the monitoring form I provide at the end of this chapter, which offers space to note the consequences of each habit area. Then share it with your provider.

Cues That It's Time to Take Your Medication

No matter the frequency, whether you take it once or twice a day, most people take medication in the morning. This can be challenging when mornings are usually harried as you get yourself, your partner or spouse, and perhaps children out the door. Time is not a luxury you have. So if you don't have a cue in place to trigger this healthy habit, it can be very hard to both remember to take it and remember that you took it. Of course, neither skipping nor double dosing are good things to do.

Keep the Container Visible: Have the cue be seeing the pill bottle itself. Make it visible. I finally got my husband in the habit of taking his morning antacid by leaving the bottle out on the kitchen counter. He sees it and takes it before he walks out the door for work. When we're on vacation, the physical setup is different so there's no visual cue. This is when we use another strategy, which I'll cover below.

Use a Pillbox: Simple pillboxes have seven compartments that you can sort your medication into: one for each day of the week. Using one can serve double duty. Not only is the pillbox itself a visual cue to prompt you, it also helps you double check that you took your medication. How many times have you taken your meds while thinking about a thousand other things and then later wondered, "Did I take them?" All you need to do is peek in that day's compartment. You may be more successful if the pillbox is somewhere that's easy to see. Or you can combine this suggestion with other cues to remind you to take the pillbox out in the first place.

Link It with an Activity: Your cue can be another activity that you never forget to do, like brushing your teeth or preparing your morning coffee or tea. Walk into the bathroom, brush your teeth, take your medication. Walk into the kitchen, turn on the kettle, pour water, take your medication. Try to focus on taking it *when you're taking it* so you don't question yourself later. If you don't combine this suggestion with using a pillbox, you can take your medications out of the containers, set them on the counter, put away the containers, and then take them all. You can also say to yourself, out loud, "Okay, I'm taking my medicine now," which will help you remember and ease the doubting thought you have 5 minutes later.

Set an Alarm: It's so easy to set a reminder, which can be an especially useful cue if you are taking your medication while on the go. Online and cell-phone technologies are at your fingertips, offering countless ways to do this. You could set an alarm like you do to wake up, schedule a regularly occurring event in your calendar, have it on your daily schedule, or use a downloaded app. If you take your medication with you to work or out to dinner, you also need a cue that reminds you to carry it with you. A little pill case that you keep in the same place every day can help.

Have Someone Remind You: I wouldn't depend on this as your sole way of remembering. The person assigned this task would either start to annoy you or become afraid of becoming too much of a nudge. But it can be helpful to have support—just make sure all parties involved are on the same page. When your routine is temporarily on hold for some reason, like going on vacation, you might want to enlist the help of your vacation partner. That's when I remind my husband to take his antacid because the normal cues in our kitchen aren't there.

Limiting Recreational Drugs and Alcohol

Because you picked up this book, you likely want to get unstuck and engage in behaviors that contribute to what matters to you. While the short-term effects of recreational drugs and alcohol can feel great, the effects a few hours later can be negative and problematic. Even in their most innocuous forms, drugs and alcohol may lead you to take a step away from—rather than toward—your sleep, health, and fitness goals. For example, they may make you more likely to eat a late-night cheesesteak, wake up repeatedly during the night, sleep in late, or skip the run you planned with a friend. You may also notice that the next day you feel more emotionally vulnerable, which is especially problematic if you are vulnerable to depression. And when you wake up feeling HN or LN, it is easier to succumb to the urge to procrastinate. Therefore, to the extent possible, I strongly encourage you to limit drinking, smoking, and taking recreational drugs as you work to improve depression and motivation, and to activate happiness. If you're thinking, "But drinking and smoking relax me," know I'm totally with your desire to relax, and that it's completely valid to want routine habits that evoke it. Here are healthy ways to go about relaxing.

Healthy Habits for Relaxation

Relaxation is the experience of LP, low arousal with a positive valence. It's when you feel peaceful, safe, and content. Your heart rate, breathing, and thinking all slow down. Allowing yourself time to relax might feel like a guilty pleasure and is often the first set of behaviors to go in a busy lifestyle. Modern life certainly reinforces the value of being on the *go, go, go.* In reality, relaxation helps to combat the physiological and psychological consequences of stress. A few of the many benefits include reducing muscle tension and chronic pain, reducing inflammation, lowering blood pressure, and improving concentration.

So when can you find the time? And how can you relax? Here are some suggestions. I know it may seem counterintuitive, but commuting can provide a great cue to relax. Perhaps as you get in your car, the subway, or set out on your walk, you turn on enjoyable music, sing your heart out, download an intellectually stimulating podcast, or make phone calls to people you actually want to talk to. Brainstorm for a creative dinner you'll cook, reflect on a spiritually meaningful passage, or contemplate fellow commuters. Basically, rather than letting your mind run rampant with thoughts that rehash earlier events or plan for challenges ahead, give yourself permission to tune into the present moment or even have playful fantasies about the future. A sample cue: you swipe your transit card, tap play on your phone, and away to *Fresh Air* with Terry Gross you go.

Another routine opportunity for relaxation might be to play double duty with your exercise habit. Cues for relaxation could include entering the yoga studio, hitting the pavement in your sneaks, putting on your helmet for a bike ride, diving into warm and refreshing water. Initiate these activities and away you go to the land of self-efficacy and calm, present-focused attention.

Now let's focus on what happens when you walk in the door from a long day at work and, perhaps, you might have been habitually triggered to pour yourself that glass of wine or pull out the pot.

Cues to Signal Relaxation at the End of a Long Day

Ideally, just walking through the door to your home would signal relaxation. But the reality is that most of us have lots of things on our personal to-do lists before we can relax. With that in mind, what types of cues do you need that will communicate to your body that it's time to unwind? Just as a symbolic glass of wine says, "Aaah, I did it," look for other special rituals to mark that time of day. What else can set the stage for you to demarcate the end of working time and the beginning of sober chill-out time? Like all new habits, repeating these behaviors helps you form associations between specific aspects of your environment and internal feelings of relaxation. Here are some suggestions.

Music: Music can communicate to you that it's time to relax, whether playing softly in the background or reverberating through headphones or speakers.

Change of Clothes: Just as exercise clothes can signal that it's time to get your movement on, changing out of your work clothes can symbolize taking your degree of professionalism (nay, perfectionism) down a few notches.

Special Nonalcoholic Beverages: Soda water in a stemless wine glass, fresh cucumber water in a martini glass, home-brewed kombucha, or iced tea can cue your shoulders to relax and body tension to release. Just as pouring wine when you walk in the door can signal the end of a work day, over time, so can a special nonalcoholic beverage. Just follow the first sip with a deep breath and, as you drink, give yourself space to mentally unwind.

Enjoy Your Meal: Oh, the joys of food. Maybe savoring your dinner can become the reward for a hard day's work. If this sounds like it might satiate your desire for a little celebration, make balanced eating your keystone habit.

Traditional Relaxation Exercises: Diaphragmatic breathing, guided imagery, or progressive muscle relaxation can directly induce states of relaxation. Meditation and mindfulness exercises are psychologically beneficial and can, at times, also trigger relaxation. There is a plethora of free resources that can guide you through relaxation exercises—all designed to help refocus your attention so that you decrease physiological and psychological stress. Here are just a few that can get you started:

- US Department of Veterans Affairs has sponsored free phone apps that include guided relaxation strategies, such as Breathe2Relax, Mindfulness Coach, and CBT-i Coach

- UCLA Mindful Awareness Research Center's website offers free resources, including audio tracks for guided practices

- Insight Timer is a popular free app that includes a wide variety of guided exercises

- Headspace is a phone app that guides you on a free ten-day, ten-minute meditation program

- Refer to Principle 3 for a diaphragmatic breathing exercise that you can practice at the same time, every day

Everyone benefits from having regular cues in place to drop their shoulders, let go of general body tension, and breathe a sigh of relief. As you set yourself up for success to follow through on your goals, I encourage you to let go of alcohol and recreational drugs as ways to relax. Instead, relax in ways that will both nourish yourself in the short run and curb temptations to procrastinate the next day.

Monitoring Your Healthy Habits

Now that you have read all the sections in this chapter, you are ready to identify which one will be your keystone habit. Which will you choose? In this final section of Principle 2, I teach you how to monitor changes as you start to make them. I encourage you to monitor all five areas, not just your keystone habit, because doing so will help you appreciate the domino effect of how interrelated each of these areas is for you.

Here are instructions for creating a straightforward form in your journal, on your computer, or on any digital device. You can also download it from the publisher's website at http://www.newharbinger.com/39430.

- At the top of the page, identify your "Keystone Habit," (the habit most likely to have a domino effect on other areas), "Set of Cues," (that will initiate the habit) and "Goal Behavior" (the healthy habit).

- Below that, draw a grid with six columns and three rows.

- Label the columns as follows: "Day of the Week," "Sleep," "Exercise," "Eating," "Substances," "Relaxation."

- Label the rows as follows: "What," "When," "Consequences."

I encourage you to devote a time at night to filling out the form, taking stock of your day, and thinking about your day to come. Completing the form should take less than five minutes. Then, you'll be set up to complete a *what, when,* and *consequences* for each of the five habit areas. You'll fill it out for every day of the week. Here is a description of how Craig filled the form out:

Keystone Habit Area: Exercise

Set of Cues: Walk in the door after work, change into exercise clothes, have a small snack, head out the door, drive to the YMCA

Goal Behavior: Play basketball at 6 p.m. every Monday

Day of the Week: Monday

What (Sleep): After my wind-down routine, I fell right to sleep

When (Sleep): At 10 p.m. I wound down by reading a book, 11 p.m. bedtime

Consequences (Sleep): Slept through the night and was able to wake up without hitting snooze on Tuesday

What (Exercise): Played basketball

When (Exercise): 6 p.m.

Consequences (Exercise): Actually felt HP when I got home instead of my usual LN

What (Eating): Was hungry for dinner and limited my dessert

When (Eating): 8 p.m.

Consequences (Eating): It was a relief not to crave sweets, and I definitely enjoyed my dinner more after working out

What (Substances): Took my meds on time

When (Substances): 7:30 a.m.

Consequences (Substances): Hard to tell, but I notice that I feel lightheaded when I don't take them, and I definitely didn't feel that today

What (Relaxation): Still haven't integrated this one yet, but I did fall asleep right away instead of staying awake and worrying

When (Relaxation): Didn't practice anything formally

Consequences (Relaxation): Even though I didn't relax, I did notice that after playing basketball my mind was quieter

Note that the row "Consequences" is not necessarily about bad outcomes and can include good outcomes and successes as well. In behavioral terms, the word denotes any type of outcome that follows a target behavior, whether helpful or unhelpful. You can consider how each behavior affects things like your mood, your sense of self, or your energy. The row for "Consequences" is where Craig will be able to start realizing that he feels more upbeat and more HP after he plays basketball than his typical LN. You can also intentionally create consequences, or rewards, for yourself. For example, if your keystone habit is preparing lunch at home to save money, your consequence at the end of the week might be using a portion of the money you saved to go on a date night with your partner.

Take Care of Yourself to Take Care of Life

Let's check back in with where we started. This chapter centers on the principle that when you engage in self-care, you have more energy to put into valued activities. You can put this principle into action by creating and maintaining healthy routines related to sleep, exercise, eating, watching your substances, and relaxation. A structured weekly routine that incorporates all five domains not only reduces the likelihood of illness, low energy, and procrastination, it also fosters momentary experiences of HP and LP. I encourage you to start with developing habits for one of the five domains, and then pay attention to the domino effect of positive consequences: perhaps adjusting your sleep naturally makes exercising easier, or perhaps focusing on exercise naturally makes your sleep more regular. Refer to the sections in this chapter as needed and use the monitoring form daily as you work on establishing your healthy habits.

Put down the book and start planning and tracking. When you're ready to keep moving forward, we'll address Principle 3, which will help you navigate any roadblocks you ran into when applying the method in this chapter. Because, like Craig, just because you say you want to go play basketball and have a clear plan to make that happen doesn't mean you will do it every time. One night, Craig could arrive home in a really sad mood and just want to crawl into bed. Craig only needs to imagine the effort it will take to get to the YMCA for him to instead make a beeline for the bedroom, tossing out his plan along the way.

The next chapter is about identifying and breaking down a moment like this one so you can successfully meet your self-care goals. How can you still meet a goal when you experience a strong, seemingly inevitable urge to avoid it? How can you not fall prey to excuses? The understanding you'll gain along the way will also set you up for the rest of your journey through this book, as you identify and then schedule a host of other values-driven behaviors that bridge the gap between what you want and what you actually do.

Principle 3

Procrastination Is an Emotional Decision to Avoid Discomfort

As you focused on making self-care behaviors part of your daily routine, I expect you had some successes. I also suspect, because you're human, that you ran into some difficulty. Were there times you hit the snooze button instead of getting out of bed and didn't have time to make your lunch? Were there times you binge-watched Netflix instead of going to exercise class or getting to bed on time? Now you are more aware of your patterns and are ready to identify, isolate, and break down that choice-point moment when you are tempted to turn further away from, rather than closer toward, your goal.

Triggers That Take You Off Track

A choice-point moment is that microsecond or that hour-long deliberation when you contemplate avoiding or approaching an activity. To understand your choice-point moments, it is useful to identify their emotional contexts. Emotions elicit behavior, and intense emotional responses make you act quickly. Emotions that are painful or uncomfortable give you an intense urge to escape the situation triggering you to feel that way and to avoid getting into another situation that might be similar. Clearly such urges function well for actual, in-the-woods survival. But the problem is that you may find yourself attempting to Ctrl+Alt+Del your way out of uncomfortable moments constantly and getting caught in a habit of *escape, escape, escape!*

Luckily, the situations that provoke this response in you tend to be predictable. They're different between people—what bugs you, I don't notice, and what bugs me wouldn't even cross your mind. But within individuals, situations that provoke the desire to escape tend to be similar. Think of these situations as *triggers*. The predictable nature of your triggers is helpful because, once you get a handle on what situations are triggering, you can practice responding adaptively to them. With awareness of them, you can even anticipate that you will get triggered in the first place and plan accordingly.

How Valid Desires Can Become Problematic

To demonstrate, I'll describe one of the most ubiquitous and mundane of choice-point moments in which we get triggered to turn away from our goals. Imagine that it's 10:25 p.m., you have washed up, and now you're in bed. Your goal is to go to sleep at 11:15 p.m. after an episode of your favorite show. You had a long day at work and are looking forward to this reward as part of your wind-down routine. With the lights dim, you hit "Continue Watching" on Netflix, and suddenly Don Draper is before you. You breathe a sigh of relief as you sink into your pillow and get absorbed in the 1960s world of *Mad Men*.

Before you know it, 48 minutes pass and the episode is over. This is your trigger. You think: *No! I'm not ready for it to end! I don't want to deal with tomorrow yet. The sooner I go to sleep, the sooner I'll have to wake up.* In your body, even if it feels subtle, your heart is beating a little quicker than it was in the middle of the show and your breathing has become shallow. Your mouth is now downturned and your nose is scrunched. You're feeling HN. If you had to name this emotion, you'd identify it as anxiety. The feeling of dread is palpable.

Your urge in that moment is to hit "Continue Watching" and make these feelings go away by watching another episode. Actually, the screen is counting down. In fifteen seconds, if you just do nothing, it'll automatically start. So maybe you'll just do nothing...

And then what happens? What is your behavior in this choice-point moment?

You let the countdown continue. You hit the button to switch to full screen. And you sit back for "just one more." This is the moment when you choose to keep watching TV instead of going to sleep at your bedtime, procrastinating on a goal behavior because it seems optional.

What are the consequences? Right away, the short-term effect is: *Yesss! This feels so good.* You experience immediate relief and enjoyment. Roger Sterling cracks you up. You have forgotten tomorrow will ever come. Once the second episode is over, you are so exhausted that you fall right asleep at 12:15 a.m., an hour later than planned.

What are the consequences in the morning? You are woken up by the alarm and hit snooze twice, so you are immediately rushed when you get out of bed. You can't leisurely drink coffee as a reward for waking up. Already stressed to get out the door on time, another trigger happens when you realize you also need to scrape fresh snow off your car. You're very annoyed, very HN, and feeling pressured. You think, *It's just one of those days!* and arrive at the office in a terrible mood.

To make sense of this pattern, which is an easy and common habit to fall into, it's helpful to look at why you would watch that second episode by identifying what functions it served.

- It made your feelings of dread and anxiety go away

- You work hard and wanted a reward

- One episode didn't feel like enough to satiate your desire

- You wanted to keep feeling relaxed and LP

- You wanted to stay engrossed so you wouldn't have to think about tomorrow

Do these desires make sense? Are they valid? I would say yes. It makes perfect sense that you wanted to relax and recharge. At the same time, there was something *problematic* about acting on those desires. You chose immediate pleasure over tomorrow's state of mind. You were looking out for your present self rather than your near-future self because acting on your desires by watching the second episode was only beneficial in the short term. You got to escape what was aversive and enjoy something instead—which is not an unreasonable yearning given your hectic days. But doing so set you up for the potential to procrastinate, which you got pulled into by snoozing through your wakeup time the next morning. It also exacerbated your exhaustion and stress, and instead of more LP feelings the next morning—when you could have sipped your coffee and eased into another long day—you were scrambling out the door in an HN state.

Notice a TRAP in Your Choice Point

I'm going to walk you through another ubiquitous triggering moment when your automatic urge may likely be to throw your plans out the window. This time, as a preview for the monitoring I'll teach you to do later in this chapter, I will track such a moment using a straightforward language and structure that will help you monitor easily and quickly in daily life.[5] Essentially, you are monitoring a TRAP:

- **T**rigger

- **R**esponse (thoughts, body changes, emotion, and urges)

- Action **P**attern

- Consequence (short and long term)

With TRAP monitoring, you notice the triggering situation (T) that led to an automatic emotional response (R). You then evaluate the consequences of how you acted (AP) in response to that triggering situation (T) and emotional response (R). TRAP monitoring will help you notice what sets off the urge to throw your plans out the window and evaluate whether or not the decision you make in that moment is in your best interest.

To illustrate how this works, I'll describe another TRAP scenario that may feel all too familiar to you. It's 6:10 p.m., and many of your colleagues have already left the office. You remember that you are signed up for a 7:15 p.m. spinning class and have 20 minutes before you need to be on the bus to get there on time. But you're feeling low energy, you're tired, and you are most comforted by the thought of curling up on the couch to watch TV. You log into the gym's webpage. You have 5 minutes to cancel your spot before you get charged as a no-show. This is your choice-point moment. Here is how you would fill out the TRAP tracking form.

> **Trigger:** It's the end of the day and I'm tired. I need to decide if I'm going to go to spinning or if I'm going to cancel before I get charged.
>
> **Emotional Response (HN, LN, HP, LP):** LN
>
> **What Does My Mind Say? (Thoughts):** I don't think I can go. I don't have it in me. I want to do nothing and be cozy, in my house, on my couch.
>
> **What Changes in My Body? (Physiology):** I feel sluggish, I'm slouching in my chair, frowning, sighing heavily, my breathing and heart rate have slowed.
>
> **Does This Emotion Have a Name That I Can Identify?** I know I'm LN and feel kind of flat. I think I might be a little sad.
>
> **What Do I Want to Do? (Action Urge):** Cancel the class. Honestly, I also want to take an Uber home—even the thought of walking to the bus exhausts me.
>
> **What Do I Actually Do? (Action Pattern):** Cancel class. I do manage to get myself home on the bus.
>
> **Immediate Consequences (Short Term):** Relief that I got myself out of going to class. Glad that at least I took the bus

and didn't spend money on Uber. But my head started aching on the way home, and I didn't really want to talk to anyone, so I ignored the phone when my mom called.

Overall Consequences (Long Term): Craved sweets for dessert. Felt a little guilty about skipping my exercise. Kept feeling low energy the rest of the night. Started to feel overwhelmed, thinking about how I'm going to have no choice but to work this hard and feel this tired every day for the next twenty-plus years.

Do you relate to this example? Again, it's nothing monumental. It's one choice, in one moment, for one night. It's a "no big deal" event with low-intensity sadness and lethargy.

The examples in this chapter show the kinds of choice points that you likely faced as you tried to implement your keystone habit in Principle 2. I want you to navigate them with eyes wide open. You will encounter mundane, omnipresent choice points every day, with every behavior that you want to implement. These are also the choice points that you will inevitably face in Principle 4, when you try to schedule and show up to additional activities that have the potential to move you further toward positive experiences. Even when it's a moment with the potential to create joy or a sense of purpose and meaning, you may still experience the choice point as challenging.

In this example, did the choice to go home come from a valid and reasonable place? Yes. You were tired, you worked a long day, and you wanted to nurture yourself and not push too hard. Did the choice set you up for a positive short- and long-term experience? Yes and no. Immediately after hitting cancel you felt some relief. Did you have an overall positive night?

Well, it didn't give you an opportunity to boost your energy and prevent your headache. The choice kept you focused on yourself and how crummy you felt, which freaked you out as you worried that you are always going to feel this way.

Distinguish Action Urges from Action Patterns

Let's explore what happens when you cope a little more flexibly with the automatic and pressing urge to throw goals out the window for the night. You can do this once you learn to distinguish the *action urge* from the actual *action pattern*. You do not have to comply with your action urges—which is a crucial piece in the puzzle.

Triggers elicit nearly automatic responses: your body changes and thoughts automatically swirl around in your mind. I would never want you to be tough on yourself for the immediate thoughts you have or for the immediate physical responses you have (sweaty palms or blushing, anyone?). Again, those emotional responses happen quickly. And they tend to reflect your unique life stories, lenses through which you view the world, genetic influences, and recent emotional states. The place to insert immediate control—to the extent that any of us have control (but that's a philosophical discussion for another day)—is to choose the behavior that follows the responses.

In other words, you can hit pause *right before you act*. Rather than automatically follow your urge, you can pause for long enough to take a step back and evaluate what is in your best interest. Sometimes acting opposite to your behavioral urge is most effective for you; sometimes acting consistently with the urge is perfectly okay. Either way, it is the actual behavioral choice we are focusing on in this book.

Let's return to the same triggering situation at the end of a long workday, when you want to cancel spinning class. What if everything in your tracking sheet was the same, including the action urge to go home and veg, but you inserted an alternative ending? What would it look like if you chose a different action pattern?

What Do I Actually Do? (Action Pattern): Reminded myself that I can always take it easy in class—no one sees how I adjust the intensity on the bike. I listened to upbeat music on my phone while riding the bus to the gym and spontaneously picked up the phone when my mom called. She told a funny, quick story about my dad that made me laugh. I got myself to class. I took the class.

Immediate Consequences (Short Term): While my energy level on a scale of 1 to 10 was a 3 after work, it went up to a 10 during class and was an 8 right after. They played good music. Definitely HP. Sweating felt good and I really looked forward to dinner.

Overall Consequences (Long Term): Enjoyed my dinner and felt proud of myself. Energy dropped to about a 5, but I did call my friend to ask how her job interview went. I smiled more than I expected. Was tired when it was time for bed. Ended the night feeling LP.

Inserting this alternative set of behaviors in response to the same triggering situation isn't earth shattering. But look at all the adaptive micromoments that were created by not automatically acting consistently with the urge to procrastinate on the goal.

By coping in ways that keep you aligned with your goals, you will be set up to feel like you are an active agent in a life of meaning and purpose. To help you accomplish this, I'm going to continue focusing on ways to break down your choice-point moments so that you hit pause before acting. The best way to break down these moments in real time is to start monitoring. I'll show you how to do this in the next section.

Monitoring Situations That Trigger the Urge to Procrastinate

Watching the second episode of *Mad Men* and skipping spinning class are examples of getting trapped by your TRAP. To catch the daily moments when you get trapped by your TRAP, monitor. The more you monitor, the more you can catch a choice-point moment, in the moment. From there, you can be in a stronger position to hit pause and extend the length of time between the action urge and the action pattern. The best way to catch it is to first gain insights into your triggers. I'll walk you through how to start a routine of monitoring your own sequences. You can download a blank form by visiting http://www.newharbinger.com/39430, record answers in your journal, or use any additional formats I will describe.

Please keep in mind that the spirit of this monitoring is not punitive or judgmental. The point is to increase your awareness of how your sequences transpire. What makes you tick? You may find it interesting to learn about yourself and the contexts that elicit rising emotions and go-to behaviors.

What Do I Monitor?

You react to triggering situations throughout your day. Observing one per day can be a good way to ease into it. The ultimate goal is to catch all behaviors that take you away from, rather than toward, your goals—including those goals that are effortful and, technically, optional. Catching these can happen both forward and backward, and you can start in the middle. Your starting point is what you first notice about the TRAP, then all the other observations can unfold.

Trigger: Do you have predictable moments in your day that are triggering for you? If you have a repeating trigger, feel free to start from the very beginning and note the cascade that follows as soon as the situation presents itself.

Response: Especially if you are struggling with persistent sadness, anxiety, anger, or any HN or LN states, you can follow your emotions to find out what behaviors your coping leads to. You could track when your emotion was most intense that day and use that to identify what triggered this response. Then fill out the subsequent actions and consequences. Do your go-to behaviors create more triggering moments in the future? Or do they help soothe you in the short term *and* keep you on track for the long term?

Action Pattern: You can also pick one instance when you acted in a way that you now feel guilty about or regret because you lost sight of your goal. After identifying that action, you can work backward, writing out the trigger and response that led up to that choice. Then you can describe the consequence, which includes those feelings of regret.

Consequence: Take note of the fact that you benefitted your present self at the expense of your future self. Work backward from there.

You might notice all kinds of patterns along the way. Do specific types of triggers get you to:

- Isolate?

- Call your best friend?

- Get in a fight?

- Give yourself an emotional hug?

- Feel hopeless?

- Sleep in too late?

- Drink too much?

- Stay in with a good book?

Monitoring will help you notice when similar behaviors are effective under certain circumstances and ineffective under other circumstances. The goal is to give you the opportunity to learn from your own experience and, based on those observations, to develop strategies for coping in optimally healthy ways. I hope you will have opportunities to learn from coping effectively, just as I anticipate you will have opportunities to learn from coping less effectively. Both will give you useful information for what to try the next time your trigger repeats...because that's the thing about triggers. They repeat themselves.

When Is It Time to Monitor?

In an ideal world, you would fill out the TRAP monitoring form in real time, as events unfold. And the ability to do so might develop over time. When you have only just begun monitoring, maybe it's not until 11 a.m. the next day that you realize watching a second episode of *Mad Men* had been a TRAP because you feel exhausted. As soon as you realize your TRAP, get your form and record it. As you continue tracking, you may even start to notice a TRAP as it's unfolding. You could be twenty minutes into the second episode when you realize you were just trapped. Good for you—it can be a great feeling to catch yourself in autopilot and gain the opportunity to view your behavior from this refined perspective. To foster this growing ability, I encourage you to pause whatever you're doing and fill out the form as soon as you recognize you got trapped. You don't have to rush to change the behavior if you're not ready. In the example, you could pause the episode for two minutes to write down the TRAP and then resume watching it. Even taking a few minutes to record will help you start to catch yourself earlier and earlier in the sequence.

If you find yourself totally forgetting to monitor, then schedule a regular time for a check-in. You could dedicate a period of time in the early evening when you can reflect back on your day. To get in the spirit of checking in more regularly than that, you might set times to routinely check in right after meals or bathroom breaks at work, which can be great cues to establish a monitoring habit.

You'll likely find that you want to adapt your level of inter-action with TRAP monitoring as the weeks go on, based on your observations. Are there vulnerable times of day when you need to monitor more frequently than others? Are there certain days of the week when you get trapped all over the place, whereas other days they have less pull? I encourage you to experiment to make monitoring as useful for your needs as it can be.

Which Method Is Best for Monitoring?

There are a lot of methods for monitoring. I use old-school pen and paper with my patients, giving them the same form provided on the website and encouraging them to have one copy for every day of the week. You can absolutely incorporate technology if that feels easier or more natural. What is most accessible to you and appropriately private? Here are some ideas.

- Download and print many copies of the template I offer on the publisher's website.

- Use a small journal and keep it with you at all times.

- Buy a pack of index cards. Each day, carry one index card with you. Put the completed index card in one place and replace it with a fresh card each morning.

- Use your favorite note-taking app.

- Create a new email message. Write your TRAP in it and save it as a draft. Reopen the same email next time you enter a TRAP, fill it out again, and save it as a draft again.

- Create a Microsoft Excel document and make each sheet a new TRAP.

- If you like to speak more than you like to write, you can record the TRAP with your phone. If you're walking and talking in public, to the people around you, you're simply having a phone conversation. If you record your monitoring, I encourage you to transcribe the content later that day, as it is easier to observe your patterns visually.

What matters most is that you are tracking with fidelity. Each week, you can take out all your forms, contemplate them, and learn about yourself—especially through the patterns you detect. Once you get better at catching these crucial moments, and you become consistent at tracking and reviewing, you'll find that it becomes easier to cope a bit differently.

How can you do this? How do you hit pause and do something different? From the awareness you gain through monitoring, you enhance *behavioral flexibility*—the ability to choose more deliberately before you act. In the next two sections, I offer tips on hitting pause when faced with low-intensity and high-intensity triggers because they may require somewhat different approaches. I'll also give you ideas for coping with sadness, anger, fear, guilt, or other tough emotions that are tailored to your emotional response style.

Coping with Low-Intensity Triggers

The low-intensity triggering moments are the ones you know too well. Should I turn off the TV? Can I get myself to drive to the gym? Do I have the energy to cook a healthy dinner? Should I read this potentially worrisome email now? Do I answer the phone or hit "Ignore?" Do I really want to crack open that beer?

When you feel the urge to escape or avoid the behaviors you are working to incorporate into your life, the single best thing you can do to hit pause and choose how to act—in that very moment—is to breathe. I know it sounds so simple, but that's at the core of its power.

Deep breathing induces a relaxation response in you. It can help you refocus and recenter. Breathing creates more space between what you want to do and what you choose to do. No matter how much you are itching to act on that urge, can you allow yourself to pause for five in-and-out breaths?

Instructions for Diaphragmatic Breathing

Here are some straightforward instructions for breathing deeply and intentionally to create the pause that you need to act more in line with your goals. Try it as you read—yes, now! The more you practice when you *don't* need it, the more you'll remember to use it when you *do* need it. You can also download a worksheet version of this exercise from the publisher's website at http://www.newharbinger.com/39430.

Preparation: Get in a comfortable position. If you're sitting, place your feet firmly on the ground. Relax your eyes, either closing them or adopting a gentle gaze. Place one hand on your chest and one hand on your abdomen—the area around and below your belly button.

Belly Breathing: Inhale so that your belly rises and fills. Exhale so that your belly falls and empties, reaching the full extent of your exhalation. The hand on your abdomen will rise and fall, but the hand on your chest will remain still and even. This will mean that you are deeply breathing from the diaphragm rather than taking shallow breaths from the chest.

Pace: Breathe slowly. Keep your exhale as slow as, and perhaps slower than, your inhale. It may help to keep count of your breaths. I like to count to five on the inhale and count to six on the exhale—you can find a count that works for you. Try it with me now.

Practice: Breathe in, slowly, feel the belly rising. Breathe out, slowly, feel the belly falling. *Two.* Breathe in, slowly, belly rise. Breathe out, slowly, belly fall. *Three.* Breathe in, slowly, belly rise. Breathe out, slowly, belly fall. *Four.* Breathing in, belly rising. Breathing out, belly falling. When you're ready take your fifth breath, make this your deepest inhale yet. And then release, slowly, exhaling and feeling your belly fall. Exhale the air all the way out. When you're ready, flutter your eyes open.

How was that exercise? What did you notice? My patients often say, "That was relaxing," which is a great starting point. But more specifically, look at what that means. When you say you feel relaxed, what do you notice happening? Some notice that their thoughts slow down or even disappear. Some notice that they feel less tense in the areas where they carry the most stress, maybe in their temples or shoulders. Some notice that they feel sleepy and some notice that they have a little bit more energy. Some notice that it was really hard to slow down their thoughts enough to pay attention, and that they want to take a few more breaths! Now, consider these applications.

- Can you imagine how breathing might be helpful when you are trying to slow your urge to act on seemingly automatic behaviors?

- If you are keyed up, freaked out, or angry, could breathing calm you down just enough to help you make a less rash and emotional decision?

- If you are sad, could the breathing soothe you in the moment and help you make a more self-compassionate decision that benefits future you as well?

- If you are feeling overwhelmed or helpless, and just want to take the path of least resistance, could breathing make you just a bit more alert and cognizant of the choice you are going to make?

Integrating Breathing with TRAP Monitoring

Let's think about breathing while returning to the quintessential dilemma: to sleep or to watch one more episode of *Mad Men*. What might it be like to insert diaphragmatic breathing into the inevitable triggering moment? You are in bed, one episode ends, and you don't want to go to sleep because it means that you'll just have to wake up and do it all again tomorrow. You want a little more escape. When the countdown to the next episode begins, literally hit the pause button. You recognize that this is a triggering moment, so you want to breathe before you act on your urge. Don't let the next episode start yet. Sit up in bed. If the computer or tablet is on your lap, set it on the nightstand.

1. Breathe in, slowly, feel the belly rising. Breathe out, slowly, feel the belly falling.

2. Breathe in, slowly, belly rise. Breathe out, slowly, belly fall.

3. Breathe in, slowly, belly rise. Breathe out, slowly, belly fall.

4. Breathing in, belly rising. Breathing out, belly falling.

5. When you're ready take your fifth breath, make this your deepest inhale yet. And then release, slowly, exhaling and feeling your belly fall. Exhale it all the way out, and when you're ready, flutter your eyes open.

You have opened your eyes. You are still sitting up in bed. The truth is, you still want to watch the show—breathing didn't magically change what you want to do. But you find you can delay a few more minutes to talk out the TRAP, or even type it out on the nearby laptop. This is what it might look like:

Trigger: One episode is over and I want to watch another.

Emotional Response (HN, LN, HP, LP): HN

What Does My Mind Say? (Thoughts): I just want the reality of tomorrow, and all that I need to do, to go away.

What Changes in My Body (Physiology): Heart beating a little quicker, breathing is a little shallower. My face is scrunched and scowling.

What Do I Want to Do? (Action Urge): Continue watching! I feel myself justifying that urge. It's really not that late and I deserve to feel good, I should just be allowed to enjoy one more.

Does This Emotion Have a Name That I Can Identify? Oh, it's anxiety. And I feel calmer when I think about watching another episode.

This is when you stop writing and think it through. What choice are you going to make? You're at the choice point. Now what?

Exploring Behaviors with Better Consequences

We have arrived at the final stage of getting through a low-intensity triggering moment. In the example, you want to nurture yourself. Your immediate urge is to do that by grabbing the most readily available resolution: the TV show. Since you've taken a breath and can evaluate the situation, can you run through the likely outcome? In general, at this choice-point moment, it's vital to ask yourself:

- What need do you want to meet?

- What will acting on the urge for momentary relief cost you later?

- Can you validate that need and also make a choice that supports your best interests, goals, and values?

Here I pick up the example again to show how you might answer these questions once you have taken a few breaths and tracked the choice point.

What need do you want to meet? Relaxation, pleasure, relief.

What will acting on the urge for momentary relief cost you later? I will feel more tired tomorrow morning, so I'll be more likely to either continue feeling tired or snooze late. Either way, I'll start off the day feeling stressed. Then at work I'll be more likely to express irritation or feel over-whelmed when something goes wrong.

Can you validate that need and also make a choice that supports your best interests, goals, and values? Here are a few ideas for a balanced solution that takes into account both short and long term needs.

- Make a playlist of three favorite songs and listen to them in bed with your eyes closed. When it ends, it's time to go to sleep.

- Set the TV's sleep timer so the show goes off after ten minutes. You can resume watching tomorrow night—and looking forward to it might help you get through your day.

- Promise yourself something special for tomor-row as incentive to go straight to sleep. Maybe stop at Starbucks instead of making coffee at home.

- Pick up the book on your nightstand and read until you become too sleepy to continue.

- If your bed partner is still awake, you could kiss or cuddle.

- Engage any of the strategies listed in Principle 2 for winding down at night. They can help your body feel tired and ready for sleep.

Would any of these suggestions be satisfactory? You can pick one, track the consequences the next day, and—most importantly—use that information the next time you're faced with the same trigger. Let's return to the TRAP monitoring in the example when you're in bed, considering an option, and deciding on one. You can fill out the consequences the next morning.

> **What Do I Actually Do? (Action Pattern):** I'm turning off the TV. I'm going to play a bedtime playlist on my phone with a few favorite songs that make me think of my last vacation.

Put it all together, and now you have a six-step process that you can follow.

1. Notice the choice point

2. Don't act yet, breathe

3. Ask yourself: What is the best way to nurture myself so I'll feel okay about my decision?

4. Choose your behavior

5. Afterward, ask yourself: How did the action serve me immediately?

6. Down the road, ask yourself: How did the behavior serve me overall?

Coping with High-Intensity Triggers

All of us experience intense emotions. Sometimes they're intense feelings of love, attraction, excitement, awe, peacefulness, or joy. We want to create more of these moments, which is the focus of Principle 4. Here, I focus on what you can do when you experience intense emotional states of panic, anger, sadness, loss, guilt, shame, or other painful emotions that are LN or HN.

To experience these emotions strongly is to be human. Many times, these emotions prompt you to act in ways that are safe and appropriate. Other times, even if the emotion makes sense, the immediate action urge that follows does not support your best interests in the long term; plus, when the feelings are intense, it's even harder to act differently from your urge. Unfortunately, if your urge is to attack, withdraw, or abandon your plans, then acting consistent with that urge may lead to some negative consequences and, as such, may very well feed the LN or HN emotion so that it gets even more intense. This makes resuming the plan you had for yourself before you got triggered feel nearly impossible. Putting it all together, the biggest problem with triggers that send you into intense LN or HN states is that the automatic action urge that results often leads you to behave in a way that keeps you stuck there, rather than slowly making your way over to LP or HP. All of this just means that it might take extra practice to break the link between the urge and choosing an effective behavior when your emotion is intense.

Just as I tailored suggestions in Principle 2 for larks and owls, here I provide individually targeted suggestions for two very different types of emotional responders: those who feel like their emotions hijack their mind and bodies (*emotional under-control*), and those who suppress their emotions or shut down before their emotions can hijack them (*emotional over-control*). Read through the overviews of both the emotional under-control style and the emotional over-control style, and see which one best describes your typical responses. Then go on to the sections that offer corresponding suggestions and take note of any that you anticipate will be helpful when you are triggered. Imagine using that strategy in the heat of intense emotion. Then, copy the strategy down or download it from the publisher's website. Keep it in an accessible place so you remember to try the ideas out when you are triggered intensely.

Overview of Emotional Under-Control Responses

In an emotionally under-controlled moment, you become overwhelmed and tend to think you "just can't handle it" when your emotions are strong. It might feel unbearable. You may not be thinking clearly and may be jumping at the chance to distract yourself from the feelings because the sense of urgency is palpable. In these moments, you might find yourself doing any of these things.

- Engaging in impulsive behaviors to make yourself feel better or to self-soothe, such as:

    Drinking alcohol

    Eating comfort food

    Gambling, shopping, or otherwise spending money in a potentially problematic way

    Going out anywhere, just so you won't be alone

    Hurting yourself physically

    Using recreational drugs or taking prescribed drugs not as indicated

- Saying whatever is on your mind, which can lead to fights with friends, family, romantic partners, coworkers, or might earn you a reprimand from your boss.

- Obsessively talking about the triggering event with someone else. *Co-ruminating* is when you talk about the problem, over and over, but don't engage attempts to solve the problem and refuse to temporarily "let it be" until you feel a little calmer.

Overview of Emotional Over-Control Responses

In an emotionally over-controlled moment, you may feel afraid that if you'd let yourself feel what you're feeling, you'd just explode. So it's safer to push strong emotions away or bury them deep down. You may feel embarrassed that you are over-reacting or like no one will understand. You insist that you "should not," "cannot," or just "will not" talk about the feelings with anyone else. Maybe you don't even understand what's going on yourself. Perhaps your mind draws a blank, your movement slows, and all you have the strength to do is close yourself in a dark room. You might find yourself doing any of these things.

- Withdrawing or turning away from others and the world in these ways:

  Ignore your phone when it rings

  Cancel social plans

  Escape into your "cave" or under the bedcovering

  When someone asks what's wrong, you deny that anything is wrong

Binge-watch TV

- Blaming, berating, or judging yourself because either the situation was your fault or you're stupid for reacting this way

- Quietly sitting and ruminating—that is, rehashing the situation over and over in your mind, analyzing what led you to feel bad and what's going to happen because you feel so bad. You're not actively trying to change the situation, you're just dwelling on it. You can also go through the motions of what you need to do, like getting home from work and making dinner, but inside you are ruminating.

- Quietly sitting and worrying—anticipating all the bad things that are going to spin out of control next. You can go through the motions of your day, all the while nonstop imagining what is going to happen next.

In the next section, I'll review suggestions targeted for what might help you in a triggering moment, depending on your typical emotional coping style. You may identify with either or both, depending on the situation or the period in your life. Feel free to pick strategies that may help you from both sections.

Strategies for Working with Emotional Under-Control

You tend to get so overwhelmed by the intense emotion that the spirit of these suggestions is to help you walk away from the emotion in a way that won't screw you up, whether later that day or the day after. I want you to nurture yourself in a truly loving and compassionate way so that you can give yourself the space you need, and still be prepared to transition back to your goals. This offers you the opportunity to move into LP or HP in due time. Here are some of the thoughts that may go through your mind, and suggestions for how to work with them.

"This will never end." Remind yourself that emotions are temporary. By definition, an emotion is a rapid-fire response to your environment. Emotions fade and give rise to new emotions. Giving yourself some space and time to decompress (with more strategies to do so below) can help you believe that this experience is but a moment, albeit a painful moment, in time.

"I'm so worked up, I don't know what to do with myself." Make noticing what is going on in your body your one objective. See if you can write the sensations down. It might help to consider yourself an investigative journalist in the heat of the storm: this is what you've been waiting for, the chance to notice what changes in your body when you're really heated up.

"Sitting still with all these feelings just does not feel like an option." But what would happen if you did? Could you go to a safe place and just breathe? Could you do a cycle of five diaphragmatic breaths, check in with how you're feeling, and then do another cycle?

"But I don't want to calm down. I'm right!" It's okay to let go of being so angry or upset *right now*. Your point may be perfectly valid. Can you resume the topic later and, for right now, make it your only objective to decrease your heart rate and increase your slow, deep breathing? The more you nurture yourself in the moment, the more effective you will be in communicating clearly and getting your needs met in this challenging situation.

"How can I stop feeling this way?" Your go-to strategy may be to distract yourself by engaging in a potentially unhelpful behavior like drinking, shopping excessively, or partying. Try to consider how that strategy—though helpful at first—will impact your ability to get the next five things done on your to-do list. Will your choice create more stress when you wake up tomorrow morning, making you feel even more vulnerable to HN or LN feelings? Will that stress increase your potential to procrastinate? I encourage you to nurture your desire for distraction in a different way.

Try to set your focus on external things so that you can get the emotional part of your brain to give way to the controlled, thinking part. There are alternative ways of distracting yourself that won't set you up for more stress further down the road. Here's a list. It's not exhaustive but can offer food for thought. Keep in mind that for many of these distractions, it will be crucial to set a timer. This is because when you allow yourself to calm down with a game or movie, you can still get yourself in trouble if you get lost in the game or movie for hours on end. Set a timer—maybe for 60 minutes if you have that luxury or smaller brackets of time if you don't—and when the timer goes off, reevaluate how you feel.

- Crossword and Sudoku puzzles are phenomenal at focusing your thoughts externally and activating your prefrontal cortex, which is your rational, planning, executive mind.

- Do you have favorite TV shows that make you laugh or get caught up in the moment? Identify them when your mood is level so you don't have to think so hard when you need to pick them out, and turn them on in a pinch.

- Sing aloud to just the right music. Is there a secret space, be it a basement, shower, or car, where you can just belt it out? Throw yourself into your tunes.

- A favorite video or online game can help, just watch your timer. There are thousands to choose from.

- I personally like to pretend to shop online. I don't let myself buy anything, but I act as if I'm going to. Focusing on all the decisions needed to make a purchase is very engrossing for me: Do I like it? Does that color go with the rest of my wardrobe? Is the price reasonable? Could I get it at a better price somewhere else? I even add it to my cart, which feels satisfying, but at the end I simply close the browser. Being able to *not make the actual purchase* is vital, so only choose this option if you can stop yourself. You can look for household appliances or best-selling cars, search ways to fix up your home or apartment space, or download free e-books.

- Tap into other ways to engage your senses. What feels good to touch? Will a warm shower soothe you? A quick stop at the nail salon or spa for a

10-minute massage? Do you want to work on a craft or hobby or house project?

- For further strategies, I highly recommend checking out *The Dialectical Behavior Therapy Skills Workbook.*[6]

Putting This into Practice

Here's a sample scenario of how this can work. Say you're in the car, getting ready to drive to work. But you're feeling really angry about an interaction you had with a family member in the kitchen, as you were heading out the door. You're so piping mad, your urge is to blow off an early meeting and go in late.

What if you sit in the car, don't even put the keys in the ignition, and do the breathing exercise? Or what if you pop in the keys, turn on the radio, and belt out a song or two before starting to drive? Then, after the breathing exercise or song ends, you check in with yourself to see if the intensity has faded. Not completely, just enough to let you think through what makes sense. Can you continue to override the urge to take yourself further from a goal of showing up for work? Perhaps the emotion has cooled just enough for you to do a quick TRAP review with a notetaking app on your phone. You clearly see the consequences for what would happen if you blew off work.

This sense of perspective helps you acknowledge how pissed off you are, see the trigger, and feel all the emotional effects that got kicked off—body and mind, in entirety. Then you make an action plan using one of the suggestions offered in this section. Say you play a rallying personal anthem on repeat, really loud, and sing all the way to work. Doing something like this may lead to consequences like: "I felt calmer by the time I got behind my desk and could focus," "I'm proud of myself for following through on my goals and getting to work," or "I had a great conversation with Jill in the elevator; I never would have seen her if I came in late."

Of course, these strategies can't solve the situation prompting the triggering event in the first place. What they can do is help you cope with the trigger in the moment in a healthy way that will reduce the generation of further stress and give you the emotional bandwidth to deal with it at a better time.

Strategies for Working with Emotional Over-Control

The other style of responding to high-intensity situations is emotional over-control. In this choice point, when your emotion is intense and you want to squash it, how can you instead react with compassion to your internal experience? Two core strategies encourage you to: touch the emotion just enough to listen to, and learn from, what it's trying to tell you; and take a break from the endless thinking and imagining that robs you of chances to participate in fresh sources of joy or relaxation. Here are some of the thoughts that may go through your mind, and suggestions for how to work with them.

"If I experience this emotion a little, then something bad will happen." With this thought, you aren't giving yourself enough credit. You are *too good* at controlling your behavior. Try to identify exactly what it is that you're afraid will happen. Then look back on your previous life experience to see if that has ever actually been the result of emotion. I suggest that you set a timer and, for 5 minutes, give yourself permission to sit and simply notice what it is you're feeling. Then do what you do best and tuck it away.

"I don't understand the emotion, it just feels bad." To understand a bit better, try monitoring it with a TRAP form. Give it a shot, just for a few minutes. You may need to do several forms to catch the whole sequence. This will help you acknowledge what is going on and dig deeper into what your emotion is telling you. Maybe you have a need that is not getting met. You don't have to do anything to fix the situation; just inwardly ask, listen, perhaps write it out, and then file that information away. A variation of this suggestion is to take out a journal and write in a stream-of-consciousness style.

"I need to get myself together—I should be over this by now." You might not like the way you feel, but I suspect it also makes a lot of sense that you feel the way you do. This might be a good time to practice the art of self-validation, and below is a potent exercise you can do to cultivate it.[7]

Throughout this four-step exercise, do not roll your eyes. Uncross your arms, uncross your legs, and let go of the grimace in your face. Place your palms on your lap, facing up, and practice a half-smile by gently placing your closed lips in a lightly upturned position.

1. Find words to describe what you are feeling and speak them out loud.

2. Reflect back what you just said, without judgment. Yes, I'm recommending that you have a conversation with yourself. Simply say that you understand what you just said. You already do this with your friends. For example, if a friend tells you, "I'm so

afraid I'm going to get fired," even if you don't agree that he is at risk of getting fired, you may reflect back, "I get it—not knowing feels really scary." So provide that same understanding reflection, just in response to your own pain or fear.

3. Reflect on how the trigger and this emotional response make sense, given the situation, your life history, and your vulnerabilities. Be honest with yourself even if you don't approve of the whole thing or don't want it to be that way. Let's continue with the example of being afraid of losing your job. You're judging yourself for freaking out about it. Ask yourself questions like: How does this triggering situation and my intense response to it make sense given my circumstance? How does this triggering situation and my intense response to it make sense given my characteristic coping style? Here's how you might contextualize your response: "My husband isn't making as much money as he used to, so I feel a lot of pressure to do well at work. I hate that I'm constantly worrying about losing my job, but I understand how the pressure makes me leap to the worst-case scenario." Or you may take notice that "Whenever my boss tells me he wants to meet with me, I automatically think I've done something wrong. I hate that I jump to that conclusion, but I've been that way my whole life. I now get why my boss's email set me off so much." Practice providing a validating statement for yourself, like these examples do.

4. Notice what it feels like to validate, for yourself, that what you're experiencing makes perfect sense—even if you don't want it to be that way. Notice what feelings of tenderness and compassion emerge. Notice what it feels like to be softer with yourself rather than being an emotional drill sergeant.

"I know I should tell someone close to me why I'm upset, but no one will understand." Disclosing private details about yourself may feel really tough. You may tend to think that others will judge you for your experiences. But you're forgetting something really important: when others have a hunch that you're upset, but they have no idea why, it is a TRAP for them. They start to worry about reasons why you might be mad at *them!*

Is there just one person you might consider bringing into your confidence? When you ask them to listen to you, guess what happens more often than not. That person feels useful and close to you because you are allowing yourself to be vulnerable with them. You can even set the parameters. If you anticipate that, in an attempt to make you feel better, they may try to reframe the situation in a better light or start to fix a problem that seems unfixable, tell them from the beginning what you're looking for. You can say something like, "It's hard for me to talk about this, but I trust you and want to tell you what's going on with me. I'm not ready for feedback—I need to sort things out in my own head first. Would you be willing to just listen?" In this way, you can better set yourself up to receive a helpful response and practice bringing someone into your confidence, however vulnerable you feel. Afterward, notice what happened: Did your worst fears come true? Did they laugh and point and tell you how ridiculous or melodramatic you are? Or did you end up feeling a little calmer after talking things through and finally getting those thoughts out of your swirling mind? Did you feel a little closer to that person? Maybe they just hugged you and didn't say anything at all. Did that actually feel safe and helpful, however caught off guard you might have been?

"No way, talking is just too much." Could you email a trusted friend? If you're afraid of pressing "Send," save it as a draft and decide later. Whether you delete it, keep it as a draft, or send it, writing will be helpful, particularly if you write it *as if* that person will read it. I wonder what types of apologies and self-judgments you could catch, like "I know you're going to think I'm…"

"I feel like my energy has been zapped. I can't do anything. There's no way I can follow through on my plans." This urge is so important to address because, as the spinning class example showed earlier in this chapter, the longer you stay sitting, the longer you will feel drained of energy. You need to activate your body to feel more active. Drop and do ten pushups. Do jumping jacks for a minute. Hold a plank position for as long as you can. Get your heart rate going.

Once you've done that, change the scenario in your mind so it doesn't feel so daunting. Just as the spinning class example showed you can keep the intensity settings low on the bike, you can make situations work for your level of energy. You can get yourself to go to almost any event by reassuring yourself that you have the option of leaving early. If you need to be around people, say during your subway commute, and you're nervous about eye contact, could you make it feel a little easier by bringing a book?

"These suggestions don't fit, I'm doing everything right. I keep my schedule. I'm getting the kids dinner. I'm checking in with my partner's day. But I'm just not *here*. All I can think about is what just happened." Yes, disengaging from the constant thoughts and images of rumination and worry is very hard to do. Paying attention to the present moment in a nonjudgmental manner, with mindfulness skills, can foster your ability to let those sticky thoughts go. I don't just mean practicing mindfulness when you are in these moments—I mean cultivating mindfulness as a way of life. If you would like to learn more about this, I recommend reading *Wherever You Go, There You Are*[8] or *The Mindful Way Through Depression.*[9] Here are some tips to short-circuit the replaying script in ruminative and worrying moments.

- Refocus your attention. Don't just go through the motions—intentionally bring your awareness to the task at hand. Cooking dinner? Smell all the aromas of the ingredients. Walking the dog? Look at those beautiful seasonal colors in nature. Showering? Notice where the hot water blasts your body. Getting dressed? Feel the textures of the fabrics.

- Practice doing a traditional mindfulness exercise such as observing your thoughts as they come. I like to sit with my eyes closed and picture a white room with two open doors: I imagine my thoughts in big, thick, black ink moving from one door to another. Other people like imagining their thoughts as leaves floating away on a stream. Some like to imagine balloons that pop as the thoughts clear.

- Try setting aside some "worry time." Set a timer for 20 minutes and in that time write down all your thoughts, concerns, and judgments in a stream-of-consciousness style. Use the whole 20 minutes. You may start repeating yourself, or you may use up the whole time and still not feel done. Just get it out on paper! Afterward, most people are amazed at how much more cognitive and emotional space they feel. If you want to read more on coping with worry, I recommend *The Worry Cure*.[10]

These suggestions are offered in the overall spirit that, when you feel afraid of your emotion, you can learn that it's not dangerous and that it might actually give you useful information. The more you can sit with the emotional experience without acting on it, even if just a little bit to start, the more it will naturally dissipate on its own. These suggestions are meant to help you be a little kinder to yourself and more compassionate with yourself. Regardless of how you would like your ideal self to be reacting, can you extend a little bit of the understanding that you naturally give to others? When your emotions spike, can you to turn to yourself and say, "Given that I'm experiencing this strong emotion, I want to take the time to ask what it's telling me. What is triggering me to heat up? How can I use this response to inform future decisions?" Then, when needed, take a break from the endless thinking and imagining that comes with the emotion so you aren't robbed of your ability to participate in life. No one wants to feel they're just going through the motions, and there are some strategies you can try to turn off the autopilot of your overactive mind.

Coping with Triggers Effectively Sets You Up to Thrive

I began this chapter by pointing out one of the best ways to understand your behavior: take a step back to observe how that behavior unfolded in its emotional context. Emotions can be strong and, at times, overwhelming. They can be very compelling, seemingly forcing you into an automatic behavior. This is why it is a priceless skill to step back, observe immediate reactions and urges, and acknowledge the choice point before acting.

Principle 3 has offered strategies that can help you cope with emotional situations that you could easily dismiss as mundane. I contend that such seemingly mundane moments are the many choice points that build the landscape of your daily life. This chapter has also shared suggestions for situations that cause very strong and painful feelings. I want you to grow to become a compassionate self-observer of all these moments, big and small.

None of us chooses perfectly each time. Instead, awareness, trial, and error can help you feel confident in your ability to respond to your ever-changing environment in ways that value yourself and your goals. Enhancing your ability to cope with life's inevitable triggers sets you up to live in ways that maximize your capacity to thrive. When you can acknowledge that you're freaked out about getting fired, and you sing your heart out to the *Hamilton* soundtrack and show up to work anyway, then you give yourself the opportunity to keep moving toward the stability you want in your life. Similarly, you can acknowledge that you are lonely, zapped of energy, and all you want to do is stay in bed—and in response you hold a plank and do some pushups. Or you tell yourself you'll show up to your friend's dinner party, stay for 45 minutes, and then reevaluate how you feel. When you respond effectively to your inevitable triggers, you foster the opportunity to keep moving toward the social connection, engagement, and laughter you want in your life.

Keep tracking each TRAP as you encounter it, and take note of any strategies that work well for you. I hope you've been keeping up with your self-care habits and using TRAP monitoring skills to help you consistently strengthen your keystone habit from Principle 2. If you put Principle 2 on hold or needed these additional tools to help you establish your keystone habit, now would be a great time to put down this book and integrate what you have learned so far for the next week or two.

Putting the two chapters together, you've been working on anticipating and removing barriers to procrastination through self-care and coping with triggers. Because who is going to get to the gym when they're ravenous? And who is going to exceed a sales quota when they don't know how to cope with an anxiety that says, "What's the point? You're just getting fired anyway." Continue to plan and monitor your self-care habits so that any time you skip out on a plan because you fell prey to the urge to procrastinate you can track that TRAP.

When you think you have a strong handle on TRAP monitoring and coping with TRAPs in healthy ways that value your needs and goals, then Principle 4 awaits to help you identify additional values-driven goals and then make consistent effort toward those goals. You can make choices you feel good about and draw on natural sources of rewards in your life to increase moments when you feel LP and HP. You can do this by creating a daily schedule and exploring what else you'd like to accomplish. I'll help you use your values to create a meaningful daily schedule and to navigate the micromoments in ways that ensure you show up for what matters.

When Your Schedule Is Full, You Do More

Principle 4

If you want to be productive, you will be more successful if you have activities planned ahead of time on your calendar. It is a universal truth that the less you must do, the less you do, whereas the busier you are, the more efficient and productive you are. In this chapter, I'll help you draw upon your values to brainstorm additional activities you'd like to work into your daily schedule. Afterward, I'll teach you skills to plan, track, and follow through on i nitiating these activities.

Schedule Your Self-Care and TRAP Strategies

To put this principle into action straightaway, I first encourage you to focus on the behaviors that served you well during Principles 2 and 3. You can look over your previous monitoring forms for clues on how to answer these questions. Remember Craig? I'll refer to his situation to illustrate.

What Did You Learn About the Consequences of the Self-Care Habits You've Initiated?

As Craig worked on his keystone habit of exercise, he learned that routine exercise helps him feel better about himself, more connected socially, and less worried. He found that team basketball, in particular, is an enjoyable way to fit exercise into his schedule. Moreover, he learned that on nights when he plays basketball, it naturally facilitates his progress on additional healthy habits like returning home to eat a balanced dinner and falling to sleep at his set bedtime.

What Did You Learn from Hitting Pause and Then Navigating Your Traps in a More Flexible Manner?

Craig has learned through TRAP monitoring that when he sets aside 20 minutes of worry time to sort through his scattered, anxious thoughts and feelings, he actually becomes more focused and productive. He also learned that even though talk radio is on during the drive to work, he doesn't listen to it all the way. Instead, he grumbles at traffic or gets lost in thoughts about what he must do later that day, both of which leave him feeling wound up and stressed. So he explored an antidote and discovered that his favorite music holds his attention better than the talk radio. The result is that he stays more present and relaxed on his daily commute.

What Behaviors Do You Want to Continue to Build into Your Daily Structure That Foster Momentary Experiences of LP and HP?

For Craig, exercise, balanced eating, and sleep are all self-care habits that made major contributions to moving out of LN and into HP and LP states on a typical weeknight. Moreover, with scheduled worry time and by listening to music on the drive to work, he has now learned strategies that promote LP and HP and get him out of the LN rut.

Using a Daily Planner

Now that you've identified the activities you want to carry forward, it's time to put these beneficial behaviors into a daily schedule. This schedule will teach you to pay attention to the effects and emotional impacts of each activity.[11] It's helpful to use a schedule that includes the following column headings, which you can download in grid format at http://www.newharbinger.com/39430.

- Planned activity

- Actual activity

- Did a TRAP get in the way of the planned activity? Yes or No

- Emotion during activity: Positive or Negative

- Emotional arousal during activity: High or Low

- I did this activity: for Pleasure, to be Functional, to Avoid something else

- Was the actual activity consistent with my values? Yes or No

- Was the actual activity social? Yes or No

Here are instructions for using this daily planner.

Step 1: The night before, write down each planned activity for the following day. Remember that no activity is too small to plan. Consult your schedule when you wake up to orient yourself to your goals.

Step 2: After the scheduled time, record what you actually did. For example, at 8 p.m. were you making tomorrow's lunch or were you browsing random Wikipedia pages? Sometimes what you actually did will be what you planned, sometimes it won't.

Step 3: Ask yourself, did a TRAP get in the way of the planned activity? If you followed through on your plan, then answer "No." If you deviated because life happened and you had to reasonably update your plan, then answer "No." If you deviated from your plan specifically because you were triggered into an avoidance pattern discussed in Principle 3, like not calling your family member at the scheduled time because you felt too LN, then answer "Yes."

Step 4: Consider what emotional impact the actual activity had. Write "P" for positive valence or "N" for negative valence. In the next column, write "H" for high physiological arousal or "L" for low physiological arousal. Doing this teaches you to pay attention to the impact that your behavioral choices have on your emotional states. Filling this out sooner to the actual activity rather than later will help you more, as your observations will be accurate and you will better learn from your experiences. Remember, you're coding the emotional impact of whatever activity you chose to engage in, planned or unplanned.

Step 5: Identify the function of the activity, that is, what purpose it served. If you chose to engage in that activity to feel good, write "P" for pleasure. If you did it to meet a goal, write "F" for functional. And if you acted to get out of, or procrastinate on, something, write "A" for avoid. Activities can have multiple functions, as cooking dinner might be both pleasurable and functional. And the same activity can have different functions at different times, as you can sometimes watch TV as planned relaxation (pleasure) and sometimes to procrastinate (avoid).

Step 6: Determine whether the activity was consistent with your values. Recall your top three values that you identified in Principle 1. Is this activity consistent with your guiding principles and how you want to act and grow in this phase of your life? Write "Yes" or "No."

Step 7: Record whether this activity was social or not. You can define what "social" means to you. For example, to some people, grocery shopping is social, because it's in public and they strike up brief conversations with strangers, and to others it is not social unless they take a friend along with them. There is no right or wrong way to evaluate whether your activity is social or not; just be consistent in how you answer. This category is helpful because it will encourage curiosity about your emotional experience when you're alone versus with others, and it will better equip you to identify what types of interactions uplift you and which deplete you.

Try getting started right now. Download a clean scheduling form for tomorrow, or create one using any of your digital devices, apps, or software. Use each row to plan an activity. Feel free to plan ahead by several days. Tomorrow morning, consult the schedule and adjust as needed. Then check in as you go, throughout your day. Your ability to use the data meaningfully will be strengthened when you complete the remaining columns as close in time to the actual event as possible.

Hopefully, applying Principles 2 and 3 helped make routine monitoring more natural. If you feel overwhelmed at the thought of using this form, or you try it out and struggle to complete it throughout the day, try setting three routine times to interact with the schedule.

- **First thing in the morning:** Consult the plan you made for your day, make any adjustments, and fill in any remaining columns from the night before

- **Midday or lunchtime:** Code the morning's actual events

- **Early evening:** Code the afternoon's actual events and plan the next day

As you start to use your daily schedule to integrate behaviors you liked from Principles 2 and 3, I'll teach you to begin looking for patterns so you can see what's serving you well and what you may still want to tweak. Then I'll help you identify some new goals you might want to additionally plan into your schedule. A day filled with values-guided behaviors will create more moments of LP and HP, and a full day will lead to much more productivity than an unplanned day.

Now is a great time to put down the book and start gathering data by using the daily schedule. Once you have tracked for about a week, you can start to learn from your patterns, see what's serving you well, and identify where you can strategically set new goals.

Looking for Patterns

To demonstrate how you can notice your own patterns, I'd like to introduce Sheila. Like many people, Sheila struggles with persistently poor moods when she's home alone at night. After tracking for a week, Sheila learned that the one night she really lit up was Monday, when she went to her book club. She compared her mood that Monday to the rest of her weeknights, when she ate dinner and watched TV at home, and noticed a stark difference.

What did Sheila learn from her own data? She realized she needs more social connection, fun, and intellectual stimulation. But the book club only meets once a month. This information can help her think creatively about extending similar benefits to other nights of the week. She now has a better sense of *what* she is looking for and *when* to plan it in.

Do you notice your own themes emerging? Certain types of activities or social situations may lift you up while other types may knock you down. In your journal or on the downloadable form, try to answer these questions:

- What are your vulnerable activities? That is, what are you doing that makes you vulnerable to feeling lower than your typical baseline?

- What are your uplifting activities? That is, what are you doing that makes you feel better than your typical baseline?

When are you vulnerable? It could be when there's a large gap in your schedule, it's a particular time of day, or you're doing a certain activity. Notice what causes a poor mood, the moments when you get trapped in TRAPs, and the times that you forget to plan. Because Sheila knows that her most vulnerable time of day is evenings, that's when she wants to insert new activities. She has identified *when* to insert the new goals she has in mind into her schedule. By monitoring her current schedule, she has also gained a terrific opportunity to be strategic about *what* new types of goals she wants to engage. She would like more opportunities to connect socially, be intellectually stimulated, and get outside the house.

Sam's situation is another example of how you can find patterns in your schedule. He noticed that weekends feel particularly hard. Through monitoring, he saw that on Saturdays and Sundays he has large gaps in his schedule. His go-to behavior during those gaps is surfing the Internet with ESPN on in the background. He was surprised to notice that he coded himself as "P" on weekday mornings at the office, while weekend mornings were coded as "N." This was a counterintuitive pattern for him to discover, because he had previously assumed that the leisure time spent sitting around his apartment was helpful for him. This insight encouraged him to connect some dots. On weekday mornings, he feels accountable to work, so the structure of waking at a set time, showing up to work, and accomplishing tasks gives him a sense of satisfaction. Without that structure in place on the weekends, when he is left to his own devices, hours pass when he feels badly about being so unproductive.

This information taught Sam that he would be better served by signing up for activities on the weekends in advance. He learned that when he feels accountable, he's more likely to show up. Sam consulted his values list to see what activities might make the best use of weekend time. He asked himself: "What type of accomplishment am I looking for? Do I want to give back to my community, spend time with family, work on physical health, or learn something new?" His unique values will inform *what* his activity choice will be. He has a clear sense that *when* he structures this activity into his weekends, he may reduce vulnerability to LN and instead spend more time experiencing HP and LP outside of the office.

What Patterns Are You Noticing?

Take out your journal or use the downloadable form to answer the following questions, in order.

- What are my most vulnerable times or days of the week?

- What activities do I want to see myself do less often?

- Are these activities inconsistent with my values?

- When are these activities occurring?

- What activities do I want to see myself do more often?

- Are these activities consistent with my values?

- When are realistic times to schedule them in?

- When would doing these activities benefit me most?

These questions lead to insights into how your current patterns are serving you. They also reveal the optimal days and times for scheduling new, goal-based activities. With these insights, you are ready to do some additional brainstorming as you refine your progress with daily scheduling. This next section is meant to get you thinking outside the box. I cover a range of domains to help inspire activity choices that can continue to serve your mood and motivation well.

Additional Inspirations: What Else You'd Like to Accomplish

You can use these suggestions to get inspired about activities you might like to add to your schedule. Broken record that I am, I encourage you to prioritize activities that fit into your top values for the next 6 to 12 months. So review the values you identified in Principle 1 and keep them in mind as you read this section.

Play to Your Strengths and Interests

When you choose a valued activity that also plays to your natural strengths and interests, you are more likely to put effort into its pursuit and stick with it over time. Some people will knit or woodwork or play an instrument for hours at a time, but the musician may hate knitting and the knitter may hate woodworking. If you are a renaissance woman or man, enjoying and excelling at a myriad of trades and interests, I wish I were you.

Here are examples of natural strengths and positive characteristics you might possess. See if any of the following descriptions apply to you. Write down any applicable characteristics, or circle them on the downloadable form, and of course feel free to add any items to your list that are unique to you. After you finish going through the list, I'll model how to identify activities that sync up.

Able to fix things	Generous
Artistic	Good at making decisions
Athletic	Good problem solver
Concerned for the well-being of others	Hardworking
	Loyal
Consistently kind	Modest
Creative	Natural leader
Energetic	Natural mentor to others
Enthusiastic	Optimistic about the future
Ethical	Organized
Financially savvy	Puts others at ease
Focused	Reliable
Forgiving	Respectful of others
Friendly	Self-disciplined
Fun to be with	Sensible
Funny	

Now you can combine your interests with your strengths to identify activities you might enjoy or feel good about doing. This sample table shows what this step might look like. You can duplicate it in your journal or use the blank downloadable form.

Interests	Natural Strengths and Positive Characteristics	New Goal Activities
I enjoy cooking	Creative	Invent new recipes
I enjoy writing	Concerned about well-being of others	Write letters to children in hospitals or emails to friends and family to see how they're doing
I'm an animal lover	Athletic	Go jogging with my dog

Find Activities That Bring You into the Present Moment

Some activities give you an opportunity to play or facilitate a state of flow, thereby helping you stay with the present moment in a curious and fluid manner. Think about the moments when you are seamlessly integrated into the demands of an activity. When do you find yourself experiencing a sense of creativity, effortlessness, and total concentration? Rather than reviewing past events in your mind or imagining what will happen in the future, when are you absorbed in the task at hand? List the activities that bring you into the present moment this way.

As you think about activities to cultivate that bring you into the present moment, refer to your daily monitoring to take note of any times when the opposite happens and you fall prey to distraction, rumination, or avoidance. For example, during your commute home from work are you:

- Singing your heart out to the radio (HP)?

- Intellectually stimulated by public radio or a book on tape (LP)?

- Laughing to Howard Stern (HP)?

- Rehashing that afternoon's meeting (LN)?

- Worrying about all the things remaining on your to-do list (HN)?

Identify the times when you want to schedule a present-moment activity to combat predictable rumination or worry that inevitably triggers LN or HN states.

Cultivate Gratitude and Positive Expectations

I encourage you to schedule time to fantasize about good experiences, think about what you are looking forward to, recall fond memories, or reflect on topics that inspire gratitude. But that may be easier said than done. Particularly if you're feeling depressed, it may be difficult to cultivate gratitude for the things you appreciate, recall events as having gone well, or anticipate that things will go well in the future. Here are some tips that may help.

Have a Conversation: You can try to reflect on these topics with a trusted other. A trusted other can help catch when you fall into the "I suck, life sucks" script and reorient you back to a more hopeful perspective. Does anyone who can do this come to mind? What conversation topics would you like to generate with him or her?

Reflect Following Another Positive Experience: You could wait until you are already having an experience of LP or HP. Once LP or HP is activated, it will be easier to orient to more hopeful and appreciative topics. Consider taking time for this reflection after a good day at work, after a workout, or while listening to music that uplifts you. Identify any strategic times when you might schedule this in for yourself.

Look at How You Approach Gratitude: It took me a long time to realize I was attempting to cultivate gratitude in an unhelpful way. I would focus on all the great things that I had in my life, yes, but I would conflate that with all that I could lose or what could go wrong. I was doing a very anxious version of gratitude: "I'm grateful that I can see, I can hear, I can use my legs, I have my mental faculties, my husband is alive, my parents aren't sick," and so on. The other side of that was anxiety over the images of loss that came to mind: what it would be like if I were blind, lost my ability to hear, were in a car accident and couldn't walk or think straight, or lost my husband or parents. Then one day I was driving for several hours, listening to old CD mixes that brought back memories of adolescence and college. I started naturally reflecting on how happy the eighth-grade me would feel if she knew that I'd end up where I am today, enjoying my job and married to someone who makes me crack up and feel cared for. That's when it hit me that I had been doing gratitude wrong!

Consider your own memories as you cultivate gratitude. What parts of your life would an earlier version of yourself be excited to see? You can tap into that mindset by looking at old photos, rereading letters and cards, or creating a music playlist that takes you back.

Look for Ways to Build Social Ties

We are social creatures who, by and large, want to belong in society. This is a basic human drive because, evolutionarily speaking, being part of a community helps to keep us alive. We want our thoughts, feelings, and behaviors to be validated by others. We benefit from the experience of human touch, including holding hands. And we are prone to feeling over-whelmed with feelings of shame or guilt when we believe we have transgressed and might be at risk of being ex-communi-cated from our close ties. In other words, this is the evolution-ary foundation of "OMG! Is he mad at me?" So as you consider ways to build social bonds, keep in mind that not just any old social interaction will do. You want interactions that support your well-being.

Emphasize Activities That Promote Social Connection: The question to ask yourself is: What types of interactions, with what people, promote feelings of connection? This is important to identify, especially if you're experiencing depression. Feeling isolated and thinking no one gets you can make you feel more stuck and overwhelmed, potentially more helpless to change things, and more hopeless that things will ever be different. Social connection can be one of the most powerful interventions. Who are the people who uplift you when you are down? Who do you *want* to go out of your way to spend time with, email, call, or text? Then single out the people who deplete your energy or disrupt you. Keep these folks in mind so that you don't inadvertently waylay a great activity, when you could have felt uplifted, by doing it with the wrong person.

Identify Who Might Benefit from Your Support: Do you want to do something thoughtful for someone or for people facing life challenges? You might feel passionate about reducing homelessness, raising awareness for specific diseases, or helping out family, friends, or community members who could use a home cooked meal. What acts of loving-kindness might you practice toward others? Contemplate this and then research any groups or organizations you might join to improve the lives of others. You may have already generated ideas for this as you worked with your values in Principle 1. Now you can see that activities like this bring the additional benefit of increasing your sense of connectedness.

Prioritizing Your New Activities

Once you have gathered these additional ideas for what you'd like to see yourself accomplish, it's time to prioritize a few that you can add to your daily schedule. Which ones are best to prioritize? When in doubt, note which activities are most consistent with your values that you are prioritizing in the next 6 to 12 months. Also, an activity may have surfaced that supports your well-being in several different ways. For example, if calling your sister more often arose as a way to enjoy your commute, connect with others, and give support to someone, that is a solid indication that the activity would be great to prioritize.

Tips to Help You Get Going

There are additional strategies you can use to successfully schedule and do new activities. This section offers tips to boost the likelihood that you will plan them and then follow through on them.

Make Each Goal as Specific as Possible

It's common to have a goal that reads something like this: "Spend more time with my family." But you may get stuck, feel overwhelmed, and procrastinate on such a goal. Why? Because it's nebulous. It is more helpful to take a general goal and then break it down further into concrete, manageable action items you can do right away. Here are some examples of action items that are consistent with the goal to spend more time with family. You can create a similar table in your journal or use the downloadable form to practice making your goals more specific.

Action Item	When to Schedule It
Ask spouse out on a date for Saturday night	7 p.m. Thursday during dinner conversation
Email sibling to schedule a video chat date	9 p.m. Tuesday
Call cousin to invite him to visit this summer	8:30 p.m. Wednesday

Once It's on Your Calendar, Imagine Yourself Following Through

Vast amounts of data suggest that imagining yourself performing actions enhances your actual performance. Athletes and musicians regularly practice "in their minds." Marsha M. Linehan, a guru of clinical psychology and expert with patients who get sidetracked by overwhelming emotions, calls this strategy "coping ahead." You can cope ahead by imagining yourself enacting the steps you lay out on your schedule while being realistic about barriers that may make it hard to follow through. In your mind, see yourself coping with those obstacles. For every new activity that you put on your schedule, try it out first by practicing the follow-through in your mind.

Use Behavioral Principles to Your Advantage

There are four behavioral principles that you can apply to scheduling and following through on goal activities. These strategies are like extra credit on a hard exam. Try them out—you won't lose any points for trying, and it's likely the payoff will be high.

1. Use Preferred Activities to Get Those You Dread Done: One of my favorite behavioral principles is the Premack Principle, which refers to using your preferred, high-frequency activities to increase the likelihood that you will engage in new or less desired goal activities. Here's an example of the principle at play. After a long day at work, I come home and still need to take care of some time-sensitive emails, which of course I'm not in the mood to do. This is my less desirable activity. It's a more desirable activity to sit on the couch with my husband and watch a show that makes us crack up. I apply the Premack Principle by making my TV watching contingent upon spending an hour finishing up those work emails. In other words, I don't let myself get on that couch until the last email is complete. Only then do I enjoy my highly desired TV time.

2. Set Up Routine Rewards: Positive reinforcement is the little nugget of reward that keeps you trucking along toward your goals. I highly encourage you to plan realistically and build in reinforcements for yourself. Reinforcement can be incredibly mundane—your brain won't mind. I often spend hours writing, so my most effective strategy is to set the timer on my phone for 35 minutes. I write for that allotted amount of time with no e-mail checking, and my cell-phone silenced and turned over. Then, when the alarm goes off, that is my planned time to reward myself: I check my email, make a hot beverage, stretch my legs, or take a bathroom break. I told you, rewards can be incredibly mundane. But they work because they help me sit down for another work period since I know another rewarding break will be waiting for me in just 35 minutes. While it can be tempting to set a grueling goal, it is unrealistic because you'll simply feel overwhelmed and procrastinate. Try a more middle-of-the-road approach by rewarding yourself for progress along the way.

3. Make the Aversive Less Aversive: If you're depressed, it's easy to imagine that an activity you have to take care of will take high amounts of effort and be highly unpleasant. That's the depression talking. Try to override the temptation to let a TRAP get in the way by making the task slightly more enjoyable or, if not more enjoyable, less aversive. Can you soften your environment to make the job feel just a little easier? For example, when I'm stuck working on long reports at work, I kick off my shoes and play good music in the background. Recall that Principle 2 is filled with examples for finding ways to ease into, or reframe, tasks that you don't look forward to doing, such as waking up and getting out of bed in the morning.

4. Strengthen Your Cues: You can be intentional about setting the cues for any activity. Let's say you want to cultivate a habit of reading rather than watching TV when you unwind at night. To be successful, you can strengthen the cues that will help you read. Where do you usually watch TV? The couch. Okay, so then you need to find a new place where you can sit and read. How about the recliner next to the couch? Differentiating the cues is important, so the first time you start your reading habit—with great intention—sit in the recliner and read. When you read the next night, read in the recliner and not on the couch. Keep repeating at the same time, in the same location. Eventually, you will likely find that it's natural to situate yourself in your chair and pick up your book at night to read.

Here's a quick review of these advanced tips:

1. Make the activity you want to do contingent upon what you're more likely to avoid (*Premack*)

2. While working on the activity you wanted to avoid, take planned breaks to give yourself a burst of pleasure, which you will be craving (*set up routine rewards*)

3. Make the activity you wanted to avoid pleasurable, and if that's not realistic, at least minimize how aversive it is (*make the aversive less aversive*)

4. If it's a behavior that you'd like to repeat, then when you show up, do it in the same space and at the same time, so that the location itself triggers the behavior (*strengthen cues*)

Advice for Having Difficulty Scheduling in the First Place

For those of you who say, "I like to be spontaneous and I don't want to plan my life," know this: showing up requires planning an activity ahead of time and scheduling it. You're very unlikely to show up for something that requires effort if you don't have a plan in place to do so. Most of us crave freedom, yet without structure we fall apart. As the guiding principle of this chapter states, it is true that the busier we are, the more efficient and productive we are. It's also true that the more flexibility there is in our schedules, the more we tend to meander and the less we tend to accomplish.

Keep in mind that you can fill your schedule with enjoyable activities. If your value is taking time for relaxation, you can schedule in a bubble bath, shopping with a friend, or going out to an enjoyable meal. A busy schedule need not be synonymous with a boring or grueling schedule. A full schedule simply means that you have direction to help you initiate activities that might activate happiness throughout the day.

Tips for Having Difficulty Following Through

You may say, "I'll follow through when I feel motivated...I'm just not motivated yet." If you wait to be moved by motivation, you are stuck in a TRAP. Many people procrastinate at home but not at work, and you may be similar. My guess is that's because at work the whole team might suffer from your procrastination, but at home the only person who will suffer from procrastination is you. So you throw your future-self under the bus to avoid temporary discomfort. This is a universal TRAP that we all fall into, as I discussed in Principle 3. For example, when are you going to *feel like* calling your insurance company because the Explanation of Benefits doesn't look right? Unless you have a plan in place to get it done, the spirit is 99 percent not going to move you to call. You'll keep feeling better in the moment, with a plan to do it later, but it won't get done. Instead, motivate yourself with a reward for doing it like watching the latest episode of your favorite TV show afterward.

Also keep in mind that when you're in a depression, anticipating most future events can feel like the equivalent of facing a discussion about the Explanation of Benefits. This might be disconcerting to you if you're equally blasé about showing up for social occasions, picking up your hobby again, cooking nutritious meals, and so on. It's important to understand that when you are HN or LN, your brain is oriented to perceive the world in ways that keep you in those states. This means that the best way to move into HP or LP is to shake up your emotional experience by doing something totally different.

If you wait passively to feel better, you will likely continue to keep feeling bad. If you instead pick up the phone and call the insurance company, get out of the house, or show up for planned activities—despite low expectations—then you give yourself the possibility of a different outcome. You might enjoy the activity more than you thought you would, feel good about yourself for tackling a goal even if the task felt terrible, feel closer to another person and more connected to the world, or feel less stressed because you got something on your to-do list done.

Finally, remember that change happens in fits and starts. As long as you are tracking with honesty and regularity, you will gather incredibly useful information—even if what you actually choose to do is off script. You especially want to track the things you did if they're not what you planned. The patterns you'll notice about yourself—like "I tend to avoid when…" or "I break my plans when…"—bring priceless awareness. Yes, awareness is the first step of behavior change. Consider discussing and troubleshooting with a trusted friend or a mental health practitioner. Keep reminding yourself: change builds from awareness. So just being aware of the times when you get stuck means you are already on your way to making the change you want to see.

Tips for When You Have Difficulty Enjoying

You may say, "There must be something wrong with me. I thought I'd enjoy that activity—playing with my kids, going for a walk, working on my creative writing—but I didn't." Consider the following reasons this could be happening and see if one of them applies to your experience.

You May Be Distracting Yourself Away from a Pleasant Experience: We can distract ourselves away from joy, whether intentionally or unintentionally, when we leave the present moment behind. To see first-hand how this works, try the following exercise. For your next meal or snack, hopefully you are going to eat something that is tasty to you. When it's time to eat, set a timer for 30 seconds. For that half-minute, be totally aware of the tastiness you are eating. Notice the flavor dancing on your tongue, the texture, the magical sensation that pulses through your body (especially if it's chocolate). Whatever you notice, just luxuriate in the taste.

Then once again set the timer for 30 seconds and keep eating. This time, as you eat think about what you're going to wear tomorrow, who has birthdays coming up, or when you need to make your credit-card payment. When the second timer goes off, pause for a moment and ask yourself, "Which situation tasted better?"

This is a great way to get a taste of your own medicine (pun intended). By only partially attending to your present experience, you only give yourself a partial opportunity to emotionally benefit from it. Your active mind keeps you away from in-the-moment pleasures. To counter this tendency, you could keep a notebook on you, have sticky notes on your desk, or use a notes app on your phone. When you have a distracting thought, urge, or idea, write it down. Then intentionally return your attention to your current activity. Plan a time to look at that thought, urge, or idea later when you can give it your full attention.

You Might Need to Decrease the Intensity of Your Current Emotion: Let's say you're feeling really intense HN or LN. You get yourself to show up for your planned activity, but you're over-the-top consumed by how intense your negative emotion is and don't stand a chance of enjoying the activity at all. If this happens to you, it might be helpful to review the section on coping with high-intensity triggers in Principle 3. You may need to carve a little time out to first address your emotional discomfort, even if it involves deep breathing in a bathroom stall, having a quick conversation with someone who cheers you up, journaling, or doing some fast cardio like jumping jacks.

The goal is to take the edge off the intensity of your current emotion so you have a better chance at focusing on, and perhaps getting some enjoyment from, your surroundings. As you take another look at Principle 3, pay close attention to strategies that might be unobtrusive and therefore realistically helpful when you're in public.

Your Emotion Could Be a Message About the Activity and Not You: Your negative emotional experience might be communicating some very useful information. Let's say you are with a boyfriend or girlfriend, taking an evening stroll on a warm summer night, and you think you should be feeling intimacy. But you keep feeling HN, HN, HN. Sure, it could be your depressed mind getting in the way. It's also quite possible that your emotions are communicating information about your needs that aren't getting met, despite the potentially romantic context. If your mood starts to improve in other contexts—like when you're alone or at work—and it stays low when you're with this person, then this might be an important message. In that case, all the present-focused exercises in the world won't fix the actual problems in your relationship that are quite validly causing you to feel badly. This point is important because I want you to remember that emotions communicate useful information, and a lack of enjoyment could be signaling something very important about your situation and your needs.

Is an Activity Worth the Effort?

You've worked through the first three principles of the book as well as this entire chapter, and you may still be wondering: *Is it worth it to take the time to plan and follow-through on activities?* In this final section of Principle 4, I want to bring additional attention to how you can gauge for yourself whether all this hard work is worth doing. First, consider your well-being. You can think of well-being as:

- A healthy ratio of positive emotional experiences to negative emotional experiences—about three experiences of HP or LP for every experience of HN or LN

- The sense that your life has meaning and purpose

- The sense that you are attaining your goals

You are now a pro at assessing the impact of your momentary choices on your emotional experience, which relates to the first point in the definition of well-being. This next section will help you consider the other two points, specifically by focusing on the impact that each choice point makes on your views of yourself, of others around you, and your life more broadly, as well as how it helps you accomplish your goals.

This comprehensive evaluation can help you navigate inevitable internal barriers to showing up to planned activities, which surface in statements like these: "What's the point?," "It's not worth it," "I'm too tired," and "I'll do it later." Sound familiar? Over time, if an activity continues to hit the mark on one or more of the following areas, you have received a major clue that it probably warrants showing up and doing—despite internal, momentary dread.

Does the Activity Impact How You View Yourself?

Quite simply, functional activities may feel uncomfortable. Let's say you were asked to speak at a work event. You dreaded preparing, you didn't enjoy standing in front of everyone, and you felt HN throughout. But after the presentation, you feel proud of yourself for taking a risk consistent with your goal of professional development. In this type of situation, focusing on how an activity affects your *view of yourself* can help you evaluate whether to repeat that behavior.

Consider a second example. Imagine that a friend was sick, and when you visited them you felt sad and LN. But it was meaningful to share those feelings of sadness together, so after you returned home you also felt good. Your behavior supported your values in friendship: to show up, be present, and listen. You view yourself positively because you acted in a way that is consistent with what's important to you.

In this way, to determine whether an activity is worth it, you can focus on how you view yourself rather than your emotional experience during the activity.

Does the Activity Impact How You View Others or Your World?

When you're feeling depressed, you not only view yourself negatively, you also tend to view your surroundings negatively. This makes the future seem bleak. Pay close attention to whether your behavioral choices confirm that negative worldview and future or, alternately, whether your behavioral choices help you view others, your world, and the future as calming, kind, uplifting, or hopeful.

Consider this scenario. You receive an invitation to the ubiquitous Fourth of July barbeque. You have an urge to stay home, but your partner cajoles you to join the neighbors in the celebration. While apprehensive, you show up. The conversation is pretty lame and the host overcooks the meat on the grill. But then you start talking to someone who just moved to town, and you find yourself chuckling as you share the quirks of the place. Then, one of the neighborhood adolescents does something surprisingly sweet for his parents and you keep smiling about it. By the time you leave, you feel a little more connected socially and a little less alone, and you consider the possibility that the world may not be entirely full of a generation of kids who don't respect their elders. When you get home, you're feeling a little more open to new social connections and even a bit hopeful about the next generation. This example shows how it can be helpful to notice that an activity makes you feel more *connected* (versus isolated) and more *hopeful* (versus hopeless, pessimistic) about the world at large.

This question can also be applied to behavior in close relationships. Let's say you are feeling vulnerable and want to withdraw into yourself. When your cell phone rings, you pick it up despite your urge to hit "Ignore" and talk to a friend, family member, or romantic partner about what's troubling you. You feel sad while discussing what is making you sad. Maybe you still can't shake feeling bad about your life. Yet maybe the sharing does make you feel close and connected to that other person. That could be a very valuable outcome in and of itself, as it intensifies your bond and teaches you that when you are in distress in a future moment, you have a safe place to turn.

You can also think about your connection with others and the world more broadly. For example, one of the reasons I like watching outlandish comedic movies and stand-up routines is because they make me feel less alone in the universe, in an existential sense. When someone does something outrageous, and I find it funny, I realize that I can't be the only one who finds it funny. Someone else created the movie or routine for lots of people to enjoy, meaning I must have a shared sense of humor with others. This realization makes me feel more connected in the world. Do you have interests that bring about that experience in you? It could happen when you listen to music, look at trees, experience art, or pray. What helps you connect with a larger sense of the world? Pay attention to anything that stirs such an experience in you. These may be moments you want to make sure to fit into your schedule.

Putting these examples together, it may be useful to evaluate how your behaviors lead you to feel about strangers, people close to you, and the world at large. If you find yourself feeling a bit more connected, encouraged, or hopeful as a consequence of showing up, that's a clue that a behavior warrants repetition.

What Is the Activity's Impact on the Actual Situation?

It's important to consider the tangible outcome of a behavior. Ask yourself, "Did this choice point lead to getting what I wanted?" Consider a conversation in which asking for what you want or saying no to something is hard for you, yet you make a choice to assert yourself despite feeling nervous. In this case, the conversation itself causes you great anxiety and puts you at HN. Let's say the other person is resistant and bites back, making you question yourself and feel burned out on people in general. But, in the end, *your needs were actually met.* Some examples: you were able to get your neighbor to turn down his loud music, your tenant to pay her rent, or your coworker to quit bossing you around. In these examples, taking action can feel uncomfortable, but it may be worth doing if you reach your larger goal—which minimizes stress and boosts well-being in the long run.

Considering the Consequences of an Activity: Short Versus Long Term

Some activities can feel all-round beneficial. Do you have a quadrafecta activity when you feel all of the following?

- Your mood is elevated

- You feel good about yourself

- You love those around you and the world

- You get the outcome you want

An experience like that is definitely possible but, as the examples in the preceding section demonstrated, it's not always the case that an activity will hit all four marks simultaneously. For the other times, when you're trying to evaluate if making the effort is *worth it*, continue to consider that the short-term discomfort may be outweighed by these slightly longer-term benefits:

- While you were engaging in the activity you might have felt terrible, yet afterward you may have experienced a sense of accomplishment

- Getting to the activity could have been a strain, and then you may have been pleasantly surprised by something that happened or someone you encountered

- It might have been emotionally tough, but your perseverance could have brought you closer to a long-term goal

- It might have pissed someone else off, but asserting yourself might have strengthened your sense of self

Take stock of short-term discomfort versus long-term benefits and use this evaluative data to help you consider the impact of your choices. And remember to consider if that long-term benefit is also consistent with your values. For example, let's say you're focused on advancing your career right now and an opportunity arrives to give a presentation, which is an HN experience for you. By volunteering to do it, you will meet your objective because it will contribute to a positive biannual review. You could decide that this outcome is more important than short-term emotional discomfort. Ask yourself, "Is my long-term goal worth overriding the short-term discomfort?" If yes, consider approaching an activity you have the urge to avoid and kick some presentation bootie.

Awareness Makes Changing Behavior Possible

One of the reasons you picked up this book is that you want to behave in specific ways. As you've seen throughout this chapter, using a schedule can give you tremendous data about your own life. In particular, you've gained excellent practice doing the following:

- Intentionally planning activities and scheduling them

- Noting on your schedule *if* you followed through

- Recognizing the consequences of each choice point

This monitoring is a fabulous habit to cultivate. Why? I'll say it again and again and again—the best way to change behavior is to monitor it! I hope that you're finding a rhythm of daily planning and monitoring that helps you be intentional about your choices while staying appropriately flexible to the unpredictable nature of all our lives. To help you be successful, I have offered lots of suggestions to fit your personal style and daily rhythm. It is up to you to take these suggestions and experiment with creating your unique daily routine.

From here on, I strongly encourage you to keep up the daily planning and follow-through. As needed, go back to the goal activities you brainstormed throughout the chapter and continue to schedule them. I want you to nurture your habit for planning activities that promote your psychological and physical health like the ones discussed in Principle 2. Keep working with the suggestions in Principle 3 for how to manage challenging emotions that might make goal completion difficult. And keep working toward a life that is consistent with your values, which is at the heart of Principles 1 and 4.

Still, even with all of this work and in spite of the best-laid plans, *it's still not easy*. There are 1,440 minutes or 86,400 seconds in a day—that's a lot of micromoments to navigate! To offer continued support, in the final chapter I teach you one specific strategy that may give you the additional boost you need to plan and follow through on the behaviors that matter most to you.

Principle 5   Stay On Track by Sharing Momentary Victories

Instead of just metaphorically patting yourself on the back when you succeed at your goals, tell others for a real pat on the back! Why? As you've likely noticed throughout your participation with this book, your emotions and behaviors do not occur in a vacuum. Your social interactions can amplify how you feel about a given situation and your corresponding behaviors, in turn. Just as others can trigger you and take you further from your goals, they can also set you up to feel more uplifted as you approach your goals.

Why are relationship events so impactful? As briefly addressed in Principle 4, we are a tribal species. Evolutionarily, it is in your best interest to form strong bonds, and your emotions send loud signals when those bonds are threatened or you perceive that they're threatened. In modern times, this might happen because you are in conflict, didn't act according to social norms, didn't hold up your end of a bargain, and so on.

Positive emotions are elicited when you feel accepted and cared for by other members of your group.

Because relationship events have such a strong influence on your emotions and behavior, in Principle 4 I encouraged you to identify social contexts that you experience as uplifting and social contexts you experience as depleting. The more uplifting interpersonal moments you have, the greater the likelihood is that you:

- Experience positive emotions (you feel good when people like you)

- Follow through on urges to activate natural sources of reward (more joy, more intense urges to be active)

- Continue to experience satisfaction and meaning that can lead to enhanced well-being (as you accomplish goals, you gain confidence)

The more interpersonally depleting moments you have, the greater the likelihood that you:

- Experience negative emotions (you feel really bad when relationships go awry)

- Act on urges to withdraw (intensified sadness leads to more intense urges to avoid)

- Continue to experience feelings of isolation and sadness that can lead to depression (your avoidance takes you deeper into isolation and sadness)

To put it as simply as possible: positive relationship events promote experiences of HP and LP, and negative relationship events promote experiences of HN and LN. In this final chapter, I teach you to get the most out of your activation goals by celebrating your momentary success experiences with others. These conversations have a host of implications for your mood, sense of self, and feelings of closeness in your relationships—all experiences that can keep you feeling HP and LP and staying on track as you progress on your path of behavior change.

Capitalize on Your Successes with Social Interactions

Think about one of the first things you do when something good happens to you. It could be something big, like your website hits the million-visitor mark. It could also be something small, just a moment when your mood brightened, even for a few seconds or minutes. Perhaps you read a mentor's flattering recommendation letter. You tried a new exercise class and, even though it was hard, you stuck it out. You made flatbread pizza with a cauliflower crust (yes, I highly recommend it). What do you usually do next?

You most likely tell someone about it. Maybe you forward the recommendation letter to your parents. Maybe you tell your coworker how sore you are from last night's workout. Maybe you post your cauliflower flatbread on Instagram with the hashtag #cauliflowercreation. (Does that hashtag exist? It should.)

When you tell someone about your uplifting experience, you are doing what two of my favorite researchers, Harry T. Reis and Shelly L. Gable, call *capitalizing.* You can capitalize on events big and small with a roommate, friend, colleague, romantic partner, parent, sibling, acquaintance, or even a stranger. And if the person you share with responds in a way that communicates interest, enthusiasm, and that they truly understand why this matters to you, then some powerful things happen. You're more likely to:

- **Experience a mood boost during that conversation.** The conversation itself becomes an uplift. And yes, even if you've been feeling depressed, having a conversation about something you're pleased with, and receiving an engaged and supportive response, has been empirically shown to improve mood.

- **Feel close to that person.** These conversations can set cornerstones for building intimacy in relationships, which are perceiving that other people understand you, care about you, and validate why you feel the way you feel. (Who would have thought talking about cauliflower could be so powerful?)

- **View the uplifting moment as even more significant than you did initially.** When the person reflects back to you how great it is, you start processing the event more deeply, perhaps identifying, "Yeah, it really *is* something!"

- **Remember that the good thing happened.** Think about your future self, who may not always be so great at recalling all the positive stuff. It's much easier to remember the tasks you didn't finish and the work you produced that wasn't "good enough." If you have this type of conversation, later you are more likely to remember that your positive event happened in the first place.

Ways Capitalization Happens

If you work with a psychologist or other mental health practitioner, he or she likely capitalizes with you regularly. Your therapist celebrates your behavioral successes and, if they're anything like me, literally gives you a high five when you do something that makes you feel proud.

You can absolutely have these conversations with other members of your support system, too. Imagine telling someone in your life about:

- Progress you made on one of the goals you've been working on as you read this book

- A tough moment that you handled with ease

- Something you're actually excited about (yes, you who started off reading this book feeling down or blasé about most things)

When you have a conversation that genuinely makes you light up inside, you may be conjuring an *active-constructive response*. This is a response that is enthusiastically supportive. In honor of my dear friend and colleague who so naturally exhibits "full-body enthusiasm" when I tell her about something good in my life, I'll refer to our capitalization buddy as Jen. With her active-constructive responses, what she communicates nonverbally is just as important as what she says. Jen smiles widely, nods, makes consistent eye contact, and keeps an open posture (with, of course, occasional high fives).

What does she say that expresses such excitement and enthusiasm about the positive events people share with her? There are three main topics that she covers.

"Tell Me More!" She Asks Questions About the Event: Jen will ask you to elaborate, and you get to re-experience what happened by fleshing out the details. She asks questions like: "What exactly did you do? Catch me up!" "What was the best part?" "Snapshot moment?" "What were you thinking?" "How were you feeling?" "What made you want to do that?"

"What Does That Mean to You?" She Encourages You to Elaborate on the Meaning of the Event: Jen is asking you to reflect on how a positive event has affected your sense of self. Such reflection can be quite powerful. Take the time to ask people this question, and you'll be surprised by what they say. And you'll be even more surprised to hear what you come up with when someone poses it to you. What does it feel like to reflect on what your goal-consistent behavior means for your life? It can feel great.

"What Are the Implications?" "What's Different Because of This?" She Probes the Consequences: Essentially, Jen is asking how this present event might influence your future. This is a question that we forget to ask others in daily life, they forget to ask us, and we forget to ask ourselves. With our friends and family, it's not a frequently posed question, yet it's one of the most critical for synthesizing information and learning from past experiences. How might this moment impact your future moments?

Think about what your conversations sound like. Consider the stories you tell after a long day of work or school. Which daily experiences are shaping your narrative: Is it a narrative centered on growth, courage, and change? Or failure, not being good enough, and pessimism?

When Capitalization Interactions Are Not Optimally Supportive

As you've been reading about the benefits of capitalization, you may be thinking to yourself, "But my mom, dad, sister, coworker, romantic partner, or roommate is not like Jen! This isn't going to work for me." It's true that not everyone will give you full-body enthusiasm. And sometimes a person can respond supportively one day but not the next. Because of this reality, I'll discuss the full range of responses you might get when you try to talk about something good that happened to you. When you understand and anticipate how your interaction partner is likely to react, you can better identify who will be most responsive to you and your needs.

Eeyore Response: Sometimes your interaction partner just can't muster the necessary enthusiasm, despite genuinely standing behind you. Quiet, understated support, referred to as a *passive-constructive response*, has been shown time and again to be, well, not good enough. A passive-constructive response is one in which you might perceive that Eeyore has a positive attitude toward the event, but he says very little or is silent about it. This might happen in a pleasant, short, or quiet exchange. A passive-constructive response does not include questions about the event, comments on the personal meaningfulness of the event, or requests for elaboration on the event's implications. It's the equivalent of "That's great" with little to no inflection, or a tepid "That's nice, dear." You are likely to hear him say something objectively supportive but that fails to engage you or get you to elaborate further. Even though Eeyore means it genuinely, the conversation is often closed at that point. Nonverbally, he could slouch, yawn, fidget, or avoid eye contact while you're talking about it. In the age of constantly present mobile devices, you might see Eeyore continue to write his e-mail as you tell him your news.

Anxious Parent Response: Sometimes your interaction partner, without skipping a beat, starts to point out all the things that could go wrong and all the possibilities you have yet to consider. It goes without saying that giving negative feedback, referred to as an *active-destructive response*, is pretty harmful. The Anxious Parent might be attentive and involved in the conversation but immediately point out the problems. Essentially, the Anxious Parent reframes the event less favorably than you did and minimizes the event's significance. You can often predict who may be likely to do this. Perhaps someone who is affected by the event and doesn't like it will counter with all the downsides. For example, if you get a fabulous job offer that requires you to move far away from your parents, siblings, or dear friends, they might not be immediately supportive. Perhaps it's in a city where your spouse doesn't want to live, so your news instigates worry. Another example is when the person you're telling is competitive with you and feels threatened by your success. His or her response may be aimed at deflating you and undermining your role in the success. And, of course, if the person means well but is a worrier in general, you may hear a response that expresses all the uncertainties that await. Whether intentional or not, an active-destructive response is a balloon popper.

The "Aren't We Still Talking About Me?" Response: Sometimes your interaction partners, without skipping a beat, just continue talking about themselves. This is the third and final no-no: your interaction partner ignores the event and doesn't engage in the conversation you want to have. This is referred to as a *passive-destructive response* and can be accomplished in one of two ways, both of which convey little or no interest in the event or the implications of the event. The "Aren't We Still Talking About Me?" person could immediately change the subject to discuss something completely different like "So, what are you doing this weekend?" Secondly, he or she could instead direct the conversation to something that happened to him or her. If you are proud that you actually made it to the pool to swim laps, she might say, "I've walked 12,000 steps for three days straight." Do you have a friend like this? It can be maddening. Growing up, my sisters and I were constantly clamoring for who was speaking and being listened to—we even had hand signals that indicated, "Spotlight is on me! Don't steal my turn yet!" We all have those acquaintances, friends, or coworkers who don't know how to listen and instead start talking about themselves, perpetually returning the spotlight to them. It's one thing when the person is a sibling and you can tease him or her into submission so they'll listen. When an "Aren't We Still Talking About Me?" person is a friend or colleague, good luck getting any thoughtful, probing questions about this event and its implications for your future.

Please remember that we all have people in our lives who consistently offer suboptimal responses, and we all have people in our lives who respond this way *sometimes*. We may even be guilty of it ourselves at times. Identifying people in your life as passive or destructive responders does not condemn these relationships. We are all human, and they may well be navigating their own TRAPs that prevent them from mustering genuine interest and excitement at times. Because of their humanness,

I want you to think through the range of responses you often receive. I want you to do so because, as you plan to capitalize on your behavioral successes, you'll want to keep in mind who can really listen to you—and when.

Identifying the Response Styles of People in Your Life

Take out your journal or use the downloadable form to write down answers to the following questions.

- **Who is at the top of your capitalization list?** You can consistently turn to this person, who won't think you're bragging and who loves to reflect with you about your momentary triumphs.

- **Who is sometimes a very supportive responder but has a few blind spots?** This could be a friend who you can celebrate most things with, except that one topic that he or she is sensitive about. It could be a romantic partner you need to approach at the right time, as he can give you enthusiasm as long as he's not "hangry" or watching a basketball game.

- **Who do you need to steer clear from when it comes to sharing important milestones?** You might identify each of their styles as one or more of the three styles described in the previous section. (And keep in mind that were you to buy them this book as a present, it comes with the added benefit that reading about the type of response you want to receive also teaches how to provide it.)

Capitalizing on Your Progress, Step by Step

Here's how to capitalize on your day-to-day choice points and keep stacking the odds in your favor that you will continue to make choices that uplift and encourage you. Again, record your reflections in your journal or on the downloadable form as you proceed through these eight steps.

1. **Call to mind the behaviors you want to keep reinforcing.** What events do you want to increase the likelihood of taking place in your daily life?

2. **Pay attention to the choice points that facilitate that goal.** If your target is to actually use that gym membership you keep paying for, then what behaviors are you engaging in that will set you up to make it there? Did you make sure you went to bed before midnight so you wouldn't be too tired the next morning? Did you pack a nutritious lunch and snack so you wouldn't be ravenous when you went after work? Did you remember to bring your gym clothes with you? Did you show up as planned?

3. **Notice that you did these things.** It is easy to overlook your micromoments of progress! Hopefully routine monitoring has been helping you notice the choice-point moments that serve you well. Keep up the good work noticing. (And then keep noticing.) Can you write down some recent examples?

4. **Think about who you want to be your capitalization buddy.** Try your best to pick the right partner based on the topic and the timing.

- **Consider the content.** Is this an okay topic to share with this person? Does it threaten them in any way? Will it be hurtful? Is this a context in which you would come off as insensitive or bragging? Is this a context in which they have their own blind spots, so they won't give you what you need?

- **Consider the timing.** Can this person usually give you what you need but is too tired, preoccupied, or stressed right now? Is this someone you can text, "Call me when you can, I have good news," and you can trust that, when they have the time to listen, they'll get back to you?

5. **You may have to let go of your hesitation.** If you ask yourself "Isn't this bragging?" I want to encourage you to experiment. That's the spirit of this book, right? If it feels uncomfortable to tell someone else about progress you're making and about momentary uplifts throughout your day, there is a chance doing so challenges some tough notion you have about yourself. If you celebrated yourself a little bit, what personal rule would you be breaking?

6. **Set yourself up to get the form of feedback that will be most encouraging to you.** Do you have the conversation via text? Email? Phone call? In person? Other forms of communication I'm not cool enough to keep up with? Any form of interaction is a venue to capitalize, though they each have advantages and limitations.

- Text messaging may bring you an immediate supportive response, but you may not be elaborating as much as you would when e-mailing or speaking

- With e-mailing, you might elaborate the most, but you miss out on a real-time conversation

- Phone calls or in-person dialogue might feel the most rewarding, but sometimes the person you want to tell isn't around until weeks or months after the event.

Consider what works best for you. Ultimately, a combination of communication modes will be most feasible.

- **Start the conversation with whatever works for you.** "I'm so excited!" "Dude, guess what?" "Want to know what happened to me today?" Use whatever language is authentic for you and fits the person you're telling.

- **Rinse and repeat!** That is:

  - Plan the behavior that is consistent with your goals

  - Be aware of that behavior

  - Pick the right person to tell given the contextual factors involved, especially content and timing

  - Tell them!

Go for it. Have your first interaction and then jot down some notes in your journal, or on the downloadable form, about how it went. What felt awkward? What felt terrific? What did you learn about yourself? What type of response did you get? What do you want to try next time?

I suspect you will find that the conversation is truly the easy part. The trick is that you need to keep paying attention to what you're doing, those micromoments that match your goals. You want to capitalize on those moments when your present self is looking out for your future self, when you are tapping into your own wisdom as a guide for your behavior.

It is my hope that building a routine of healthy habits in Principle 2, catching and identifying your TRAPs in Principle 3, and creating a full schedule of meaningful activities in Principle 4 will give you lots of opportunities for capitalizing. Keep in mind that your capacity to capitalize on your personal goals may provide much-needed encouragement and motivation. Plus, the interaction itself may help you intensify your connection with your capitalization buddy. Remember, you're not calling to boast—you're calling to share your experiences as you cope with life's challenges and build a life of meaning and purpose that activates happiness.

Conclusion

We all feel more in control, hopeful, and are more likely to believe life has meaning and purpose when we spend time connecting with our core values. What those core values look like is different for everyone. We might do our best when we are spending time with family, throwing ourselves into a career path, giving back to society, being in nature, nourishing our body, or learning new things. No matter what we're doing, when we routinely connect with our own personal priorities, we are living—not just surviving. This consonance between our actions and our priorities promotes our sense of well-being and actively combats vulnerability to depression.

Here's the rub. Being effortful depletes resources, and all of us are primed to avoid discomfort. Our values-congruent behaviors require us to pick up the phone (when we want to hit ignore), put on clothes (when we want to stay in our pajamas), speak up (when we want to keep silent), try something new (when we are afraid of being embarrassed), or sit down quietly (when we want to be distracted from ourselves).

On the one hand, putting in a bit of effort pays off. It always does. Activities that are congruent with values promote close relationships, financial and practical resources, and contribute to our sense of integrity, creativity, and self-knowledge. Values-congruent activities also tend to yield positive emotional experiences like feeling alert, calm, or excited. These positive emotions in turn orient us to keep behaving in ways that promote our continued experience of these positive emotional states. And even when it seems like luck is not on our side and we can't catch a break, we can always stand behind our choice to do our best in spite of the actual outcome—which is a valued outcome in itself and likely worth the effort.

Despite intellectually knowing that a bit of effort pays off, our urge is to be comfortable *now!* Which is why we ignore the ringing phone (and think "I'll call them tomorrow"), stay in our pajamas (and think "Let me just check my email first, then I'll get dressed and leave…"), stay silent (and think "What's the point? It won't make any difference if I say anything"), don't participate (and think, "I'll never be able to pull that off"), and stay on Facebook, watch TV, or shop (because we're afraid of that still, small voice inside).

Propelling toward goals is universally difficult, and that difficulty is magnified in depression. I hope that reading this book has normalized this challenge, helped you understand your urges and behavioral choices in context, and given you a framework for becoming aware of when and why you make the choices you do. In that sense, I'll consider this book a success if it encourages you to adopt an attitude of compassion, reminding yourself that in your profound humanness, what "should" be easy is not always so easy. Moreover, I'll consider this book a success if you have simply tried to start experimenting with different micromoments throughout your day in which you do your best to look out for your future self as well as your present self. It's hard and that's okay. From your willingness to experiment, you will learn to navigate your daily experiences in ways that create more uplifting moments and bring you closer to a life of meaning and purpose.

If you take away just a few lessons from this book, I hope at the top of your list will be your recognition—from your own experimentation—that putting yourself on a sleep schedule, exercising, eating nourishing meals, taking medication as prescribed, limiting other substances, and cultivating relaxation are the backbones of a healthy life. No matter how far your mood drops, keep these behaviors going. No matter how frequently you are crying, how much you're dreading parts of your life, or whether you feel like you're in a crisis, engage in these behaviors like clockwork. The more these behaviors become part of your habitual routine, the easier it becomes to follow through—no matter that you feel extremely lousy and that your thoughts are compelling you to stay lying down, on the couch, watching Netflix.

I also hope you took away a language to describe your painful, intense, and loud emotions that make you act quickly and that often create more stress in the long run. When you put words to emotions, you activate frontal parts of your brain that shake up the limbic hold the emotional experience has on you. Your ability to write out your trigger and emotional response, in and of itself, is therapeutic. With the added skills, especially diaphragmatic breathing, you have the ability to extend the length of time between your urge and what you actually choose to do. You have a language that can help you make a choice that doesn't exclusively value your comfort in the moment at the expense of your future self.

Understanding your triggers doesn't just help you navigate a moment differently. It might also teach you that making a big-scale change might decrease the likelihood that certain triggers happen in the first place. If specific situations constantly get you riled, is this communicating something about your surroundings? Is there a chance to make a change? Understanding your triggers also teaches you about yourself, what makes you tick, and gives you a chance to have compassion for yourself. You might connect the dots that early life experiences continue to have an effect on you as you realize, "Wow, ever since that happened, I'm always concerned that..." And remember, there's nothing inherently wrong with having strong emotional responses to internal and external triggers. That's part of being human, part of how your brain is wired, and part of how your mind makes sense of your life history and current environment. You have an opportunity to embrace your reaction, own your reaction, and then intervene at the level of behavior. You have the chance to say: "I get why I'm responding the way I am. Now, what is my best option for what to do next?"

As you got in the habit of creating a daily schedule, I hope it started to become second nature to notice that you do more when you have daily structure. I also hope you started to get strategic about when and how to schedule moments that feel intuitively good and right. These moments likely feel this way because you've chosen to act in a way that is consistent with your guiding values and priorities. And I hope you have started to let it feel good every time you wrote down the "Yes" that indicates your actual activity was your planned activity, and then wrote "No" because a TRAP did not get in the way, thank you very much.

The more practice you have gained following through on your goals, the more you may have found yourself wanting to celebrate these momentary victories with others, and the more you may have found your narrative shifting. The stories we tell ourselves are powerful. Are you beginning to see yourself as someone who has the grit to persevere and the hope to keep trying?

Looking Out for Future You

Thank you for taking this journey with me. I hope you continue to actively plan and monitor as you work to make continued progress, and I hope you remember to refer back to the book and your notes in the months or years ahead whenever you start to notice a shift in your behaviors or a shift in your mood.

It is important to note that achieving a state of wellness and activating happiness is a dynamic process. Wellness is comprised of a set of behaviors that shape, and are shaped by, your ever-changing environment. In that regard, this book operationalizes a process, a philosophy perhaps, of daily living in response to your changing environment. Bumps and down periods occur—they are normal, happen to all of us, and are part of the human experience. Knowing how to take care of your mind and body, and a willingness to make choices that are purposeful and wise, will help you face a future of unknown challenges with greater equanimity.

In the spirit of taking care of your future self, set aside a few moments and thoughtfully respond to the following questions in your journal or on the downloadable form while your observations are fresh. These responses will serve as your quick reference if you start to notice a decrease in your healthy habits and an increase in your low motivation or depressive habits.

- What might your telltale signs be that you're dropping into a mode of procrastination, excuse-making, and choosing immediate comfort over long-term goals?

- What are some of the biggest lessons you learned from this book that will signal you to compassionately get yourself back on track?

- Why is it worth the effort to catch your depressive habits, reacting to "I don't want to" with activity rather than inactivity?

- Why is it worth the effort to build in a routine structure of activities that you do no matter how low your motivation is?

- Overall, what did you learn about yourself from participating in this book?

- Is there anything else you want your future self to remember about your participation in this book?

The spirit of this book has been to help you navigate your moment-to-moment choice points in daily life. These choice points are the moments that accumulate throughout your days and build into a life of purpose and meaning. I hope you have started to tap into your own wisdom as a guide for navigating the choice points of your ever-evolving daily life as you continually work to activate your personal sense of happiness.

Acknowledgments

The journey to writing this book started in many ways with Kathryn Bottonari and Jim Harbin. I went through Katie and Jim's rotation at the Ralph H. Johnson VA Medical Center as a predoctoral intern, during which time I discovered my passion for leading therapy groups. With their support, I found a way of bringing research to life in a way that surpassed any work I had done in my usual one-on-one clinical practice.

This passion guided me as a research fellow in the Mental Illness, Research, Education and Clinical Center Postdoctoral Fellowship at the Corporal Michael J. Crescenz VA Medical Center and University of Pennsylvania, where I was encouraged to follow my passion to create a group behavioral activation clinic. With the fantastic mentorship of Jason Goodson, I adapted a protocol and had the chance to work with dozens of outstanding men and women Veterans. Thank you to every provider at the VA who referred patients and encouraged me to keep the clinic running. These groups changed my life.

The invitation to write this book was a direct consequence of these groups, as I was approached after presenting the treatment model and initial findings at a national conference. Sure, the content resonated, but I highly suspect it was my outpouring of enthusiasm about the work that caught the attention of the publisher—enthusiasm I possessed *because* of the investment and enthusiasm of each and every Veteran with whom I worked. Not only did these groups open this door, profession-ally I also grew as a clinician in innumerable ways with the feedback, challenges, and successes I saw the Veterans experi-encing. Perhaps most importantly, the personal impact of my work with this group of Veterans was profound. The connec-tions they fostered with one another, and with me, deeply impacted my quality of life and belief in this profession. That's why this book is dedicated to each and every one of you.

I'd also like to thank other key mentors that shaped my conceptual lens, intellectual curiosity, and growth as a researcher and clinician. Of course, a significant thank you to my Stony Brook University mentors and supervisors, including Joanne Davila, Dina Vivian, and Marvin Goldfried. The drive to bridge research with practice was valued and encouraged and launched me to where I am today. The innumerable con-ceptualization and clinical skills I learned while completing a predoctoral externship at CBT DBT Associates is clear with every chapter of this book. As a predoctoral intern, the research support from Daniel Gros helped me connect to behavioral activation as a researcher, and the clinical support from Julian and Alice Libet fostered trust in my developing expertise as a clinician. As a fellow, I am thankful for such generous and benevolent mentorship from Michael Thase, Steven Sayers, Shahrzad Mavandadi, and Hank Kranzler, as well as incredible companionship and collaboration from Elaine Boland and Rachel Smith. Thanks also to Elaine for teaching me about the importance of sleep in the treatment of depression—Principle 2 reflects your influence! I am also thankful for one of my all-time favorite collaborators, Lisa Starr, who is helping me study the principles of behavioral activation as they are enacted in our participants' daily lives.

And now as my career has brought me back to my undergraduate roots at Emory, I am thrilled for the opportunity to continue to specialize in the research and treatment of depression. I humbly hope to continue a career among fabulous colleagues, dedicated to bridging research and practice, and learning from my patients every step of the way.

Thank you to my dear friend and trusted colleague Jennifer Sumner for comments on an earlier draft of this book. Principle 5 is dedicated to you. Thanks to Matthew McKay for believing there was a book in this approach and thanks to my editor, Ryan Buresh, for helping turn our idea into reality.

Thank you to all of my instructors at Philly Power Yoga and Thrive Pilates for being a core part of my own well-being recipe during the years in which the ideas for this book came to life.

Finally, thank you to my friends and family who capitalized on every step of this journey with me. Words cannot do justice—please know how much I appreciate your encouragement to take risks and grow consistent with my own values. And, finally, a special thank you to my loving lark of a husband, Benjamin Brewer.

Notes

1   Trevor Mazzucchelli, Robert Kane, and Clare Rees, "Behavioral Activation Treatments for Depression in Adults: A Meta-Analysis and Review," *Clinical Psychology: Science and Practice* 16 (October 2009): 383–411.

———— "Behavioral Activation Interventions for Well-Being: A Meta-Analysis," *The Journal of Positive Psychology* 5 (May 2010).

2   Alex Korb, *The Upward Spiral* (Oakland: New Harbinger Publications, 2015).

3   Charles Duhigg, *The Power of Habit* (New York: Random House, 2012).

4   Tara Parker-Pope, "Really, Really Short Workouts," *New York Times*, accessed May 2, 2017. http://www.nytimes.com /well/guides/really-really-short-workouts.

5   Christopher R. Martell, Sona Dimidjian, and Ruth Herman-Dunn, *Behavioral Activation for Depression* (New York: The Guilford Press, 2010); Rachel Hershenberg, Rachel V. Smith, Jason T. Goodson, and Michael E. Thase, "Activating Veterans Toward Sources of Reward: A Pilot Report on Development, Feasibility, and Clinical Outcomes

of a 12-Week Behavioral Activation Group Treatment," *Cognitive and Behavioral Practice*, (forthcoming).

6   Matthew McKay, Jeffrey C. Wood, and Jeffrey Brantley, *The Dialectical Behavior Therapy Skills Workbook* (Oakland, CA. New Harbinger Publications, 2007).

7   Inspired by Alec L. Miller, Jill H. Rathus, and Marsha M. Linehan, *Dialectical Behavior Therapy with Suicidal Adolescents* (New York: The Guilford Press, 2007).

8   Jon Kabat-Zinn, *Wherever You Go, There You Are* (New York: Hachette Books, 2014).

9   Mark Williams, John Teasdale, Zindel Siegel, and Jon Kabat-Zinn, *The Mindful Way Through Depression* (New York: The Guilford Press, 2012).

10 Robert L. Leahy, *The Worry Cure* (New York: Three Rivers Press, 2005).

11 Rachel Hershenberg, Rachel V. Smith, Jason T. Goodson, and Michael E. Thase, "Activating Veterans Toward Sources of Reward: A Pilot Report on Development, Feasibility, and Clinical Outcomes of a 12-Week Behavioral Activation Group Treatment," *Cognitive and Behavioral Practice*, (forthcoming).

Rachel Hershenberg, PhD, is a licensed clinical psychologist specializing in the research and treatment of depression. She is assistant professor of psychiatry and behavioral sciences at Emory University, and director of psychotherapy in Emory's Treatment Resistant Depression program. She has published over twenty-five peer-reviewed publications and has appeared as a guest specialist on local radio.

Foreword writer **Marvin R. Goldfried, PhD**, is distinguished professor of psychology at Stony Brook University. In addition to his teaching, clinical supervision, and research, he maintains a limited practice of psychotherapy in New York City. He is past president of the psychotherapy division of the American Psychological Association, and author, coauthor, or editor of several books, including *Clinical Behavior Therapy*, *Converging Themes in Psychotherapy*, *Handbook of Psychotherapy Integration*, *From Cognitive-Behavior Therapy to Psychotherapy Integration*, and *How Therapists Change*.

MORE BOOKS *from*
NEW HARBINGER PUBLICATIONS

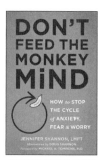

DON'T FEED THE MONKEY MIND

How to Stop the Cycle of Anxiety, Fear & Worry

ISBN: 978-1626255067 / US $16.95

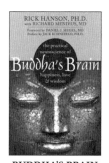

BUDDHA'S BRAIN

The Practical Neuroscience of Happiness, Love & Wisdom

ISBN: 978-1572246959 / US $17.95

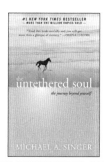

THE UNTETHERED SOUL

The Journey Beyond Yourself

ISBN: 978-1572245372 / US $16.95

THE WORRY TRICK

How Your Brain Tricks You into Expecting the Worst & What You Can Do About It

ISBN: 978-1626253186 / US $16.95

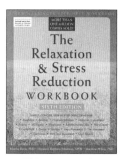

THE RELAXATION & STRESS REDUCTION WORKBOOK, SIXTH EDITION

ISBN: 978-1572245495 / US $24.95

50 WAYS TO SOOTHE YOURSELF WITHOUT FOOD

ISBN: 978-1572246768 / US $17.95

Register your **new harbinger** titles for additional benefits!

When you register your **new harbinger** title—purchased in any format, from any source—you get access to benefits like the following:

- Downloadable accessories like printable worksheets and extra content

- Instructional videos and audio files

- Information about updates, corrections, and new editions

Not every title has accessories, but we're adding new material all the time.

Access free accessories in 3 easy steps:

1. Sign in at NewHarbinger.com (or **register** to create an account).

2. Click on **register a book**. Search for your title and click the **register** button when it appears.

3. Click on the **book cover or title** to go to its details page. Click on **accessories** to view and access files.

That's all there is to it!

If you need help, visit:

NewHarbinger.com/accessories

new harbinger
CELEBRATING
40 YEARS